FASHIONIZE

THE ART OF FASHION ILLUSTRATION

selected by delicatessen

Tsuyoshi Hirano › personal work

FASHIONIZE
THE ART OF FASHION ILLUSTRATION
selected by Delicatessen
Publisher
Happy Books, Italy ISBN 88-86416-53-9

Concept:
cristiana valentini & gabriele fantuzzi
www.delicatessen.it

Art direction:
gabriele fantuzzi@delicatessen

Distribution:
www.happybookstore.com
happy@happybooks.it

Website:
www.mondofragile.com
info@mondofragile.com

COVER
TINA BERNING
SLEEK Magazine, Germany, Premier Issue 2003
Photography: Joachim Baldauf - www.joachimbaldauf.com
Beauty Direction: Armin Morbach www.ballsaal.com
Fashion: Tulpen - Art Direction: Anita Mrusek
Model: theresa / modelwerk, germany

BACK
JEAN MARIE ANGLES
The Crocodiles Inside Me
FEMINA magazine
photo by PASCALE LEGRAND

INSIDE COVER
STINA PERSSON
FlowersThisisamagazine and 2K T-shirts

Titles Type:
KAA typeface
courtesy of Janssen Design, www.bfgjanssen.de

Jonathan Tran › up in the sky, personal work

PREFACE

The secret of beauty is in the harmony of contrasts.

Thomas of Aquino

They are cheeky and sophisticated, ironical and unusual. With their charme and character they lead us to imaginary worlds, where photography is pushed to the limit: fashion illustrations celebrate a booming comeback. Grown out of representation of materials and styles they make use of all artistic devices, inspiring our senses with their personality and giving us our own free individual space. A glance at the pages of FASHIONIZE shows that illustrations can reach such high levels of aesthetic expression that the ars minor concept is not justified anymore.

With the present book, the Italian duo DELICATESSEN has succeeded expertly well in presenting a showcase selection of young international illustrators and their innovative artworks. The feeling that Cristiano Valentini and Gabriele Fantuzzi - both well-known graphic designers - show for design-guides was present ever since their first publication MONDOFRAGILE, an exciting panorama of Fashion Illustration in Japan and homage to the visual culture of this country. Originality and quality both in graphics and in concept also mark the second work: MASCOTTE! an instructive view of the sprightly cosmos of small cute characters and puppets. Their source book FASHIONIZE achieves now a **trilogy**, where the pulse of time is beating.

FASHIONIZE is an exciting journey through the experimental field of new aesthetical, conceptual and technical communication styles of Fashion and Lifestyle as well.

You'll find inside the works of 31 illustrators who, like in 21 Century fashion, refuse traditional classifications. They follow their own way; their commitments are "good noses" able to smell trend-setting brands and medias. Why Fashion Illustration celebrates its (almost) centenary by a comeback, a brief glance at its history tells us: when in the last century, with the growing diffusion of magazines, people started to get interested in clothing theme, fashion drawings had an information task only.

The aesthetic and original potential of fashion graphics was recognized by the couturier Paul Poiret, when in 1908 he gave the artist Paul Iribe plenty of rope in representation of his creations. It began the big era of fashion illustration, a prime example: Romain de Tirtoff, in short Erté.

The increasing commercialization of fashion, in the Thirties, caused photography to replace as a "modern" medium fashion drawings. One of few exceptions was the illustrations of René Gruau, who stood out in the Fifties against photography. Fashion became a juvenile and mass phenomenon. When in the Eighties the topmodel cult peaked out, the representation of perfection started more and more fading. Almost like pioneers, a handful of illustrators as Mats Gustafson and Lorenzo Mattotti opposed with their sensual artworks the aseptic photographic stylings.

Photography searched new ways beyond the traditional representation of beauty in crude daily sceneries, which threatened to dissolve, just like the portrayed people.

This reflected an increasing transformation of values in the society which took shape after the New Economy flop and the attack of 11th september. It followed a revival of stable, spiritual values and a desire of preserving identity, a sort of change of mood that also influenced aesthetics. In the pursuit of authenticity and originality some trendsetting magazines as WALLPAPER discovered the creative power of illustrators and put more and more their artworks in the place of photography. Vintage became the key-word of fashion world.

Designer's favourite was the formal language of the Fifties and Sixties with its bidimensional elegance, soft colours and smart art décor. Nowadays, slim silhouettes with passion for shopping and Martini populate inflationary magazines and advertisings. Cheeky young ladies with fancy pony-tails sprawling in lounge spaces, suggest us through their strongly made up eyelash winking their positive life attitude. Others make a journey to the future: cosmic cybergirls from Manga and Anime universe arouse a play-instinct in trendsetters. Side effect: strongly increasing cases of vector addiction. But not all of them travel with their curves in the same one-way road; they rather use their freedom, fantasy and talent.

FASHIONIZE shows the most interesting representatives of this young generation. Their art style is multifaceted and eclectic, as the fashion style they represent: romantic, technological, surrealist, minimal, expressionist, and metaphysical. There's a lot of works to see, verging on classical to abstract and deconstructed forms. It doesn't matter if the handmade effect has been created in analogical or digital. Computer is a tool, a means to achieve the aim. When asking the young illustrators about their work methods, their artistic-technical virtuosity gets clear. To be quoted from, here's the german illustrator Tina Berning: "I try to find for each project a proper language. Therefore I use many different techniques, I scribble with my pen on cheap paper, I paint gouache on canvas, I make collages with coloured paper, I use Freehand, and so on... At the end I put everything in my computer, thanks to Photoshop!"
Her trial with aesthetic doesn't take place in glazed magazines, rather in everyday life, on the street, in museums - inspired from people, recovered objects or state of materials. Very close to the young artists are the works of English and in particular American Pop Art. "The iconoclastic nature of elevating the everyday to high Art drives me", says Tony Campbell. His foible for Andy Warhol and Jeff Koons is obvious. So, the American brings the posterisation techniques in his works.
Sapient and unbiased, the new generation make use of Art History in its stylistic repertoires.
Quite explicit it's, i.e., the influence of the Viennese Secessionists (in particular of Egon Schiele) present in Stina Persson's works. Expressive force lies in the eyes and in the hands of its protagonists. The form springs from water-colours and caricature abridgments.
In parallel to a surrealistic trend, to be noted both in art and in fashion photography, many illustrators address themselves to an estrangement from reality, going inside the sphere of irrational and unconscious. They seem to leave signs in the stream, which spontaneously emerge in a creative act. An apparently uncontrolled scribble matches photographs or objects reproduced in a photo-realistic way, so actuating a creative short circuit. The artworks of the Finnish Kustaa Saksi are an exciting dialogue between the "objective" representation and the intuitive "subjective" reprocessing.

The emotionality and the spontaneity of hand drawings undramatize the represented accessory or outfit. It gets its own importance in anarchical way, that's quite emblematic for the decline of brand dictates. And it can be at the same time sublimated. That's traceable in the illustrations of Jonathan Tran "Fashion illustrations should capture idealisms and moods. Their should communicate all the intangible things that are in twined with the subject", says the Briton born in Gibraltar. Photographic projects are the base of his stencil works that he draws up in a second time with paint, chalks, ink or photographs. In particular, in the pictorially conceived illustrations you hardly recognize where the illustration ends and the photography begins. They both fuse digitally together at a common boiling point.

A consequent fact is the new direction of photography, which tries to become more and more similar to illustration.

This process attracts Jacqui Paull too: "I like the idea of illustration verses photography, flat verses 3D all fusing together. I like to push the image to the limit, manipulating the images on Photoshop", that's the statement of the young English artist. His protagonists stand like extra-terrestrials in their urban and household surroundings. Where fashion illustration gets out of its illustrating function, it can expose social structures.

The works that Cristiana Valentini and Gabriele Fantuzzi have collected for FASHIONIZE with unerring far-sightedness, write a culture history that retain more than analysis and interpretation of the spirit of time. They give the fleetingness of their products a certain eternity. In a period, in which fashion pushes more and more towards art and self-staging, only a communication bringing along authenticity and universal autonomy, at one time, can be the most appropriate. Let yourselves be inspired by the appeal of the intriguing and self-conscious signs of a new era.

Susanne Schaller

Translated by Isabella Fanfarillo

SUSANNE SCHALLER works as free-lance and Artdirector in Rome (www.bild-text.it).
She's been working for a long time as foreign correspondent for the German review Novum.

LEFT › Pierre Louis Mascia, Magnum inc, Japan

RIGHT › Dominique Donois, window display for the fashion shop "Absinthe"

OPPOSITE
Jaqui Paull › lady, personal work

TINA BERNING

GERMANY

THIS PAGE & OPPOSITE: sleek - SLEEK Magazine, Germany, Premier Issue 2003
Photography: Joachim Baldauf - www.joachimbaldauf.com Newspaper fashion things: www.tulpendesign.com
Beauty Direction: Armin Morbach www.ballsaal.com Fashion: Tulpen - Art Direction: Anita Mrusek
Models: joulia / place models, germany, franka, andressa, morgan, claudia / modelwerk, germany

12
9
3
men
#206
CHECK OUT TIME IS 11:00
结帐时间11:00点

miumiu
Allegra, Germany, September 2003,
Art Direction: Claudia Trosse
Fashion Editor: Isa Petereit

Blütenzauber

bolero_blossom
BOLERO Magazine, Switzerland

Photography: Zoé Tempest www.zoetempest.ch
Hair|Makeup: Patrick Kaestli www.makeup-artist.ch
Model: Sanrda Jahn www.fotogen.ch
Art Direction: Jürg Sturzenegger
Fashion Director: Sabina Diethelm

PAGES 16/19
vorn
vorn magazin
1. Issue 2004
Germany
Art Direction:
Joachim Baldauf,
Agnes Feckl
www.vornmagazine.com

SEB JARNOT

FRANCE

Nike campaign (pages 20, 21,22)
Fall/winter 2002
Agency: Wieden+Kennedy (Nl)
CD: Paul Shearer / Glenn Cole AD: Merete Busk
Sa: Janine Byrne PJM/PDM: Nicola Applegate
AE: Gemma Requesens
AB: Tracy Kelly
Photos: Alan Clarke
Illustrations: Seb Jarnot

NERU TANK
KARATI CAPRI

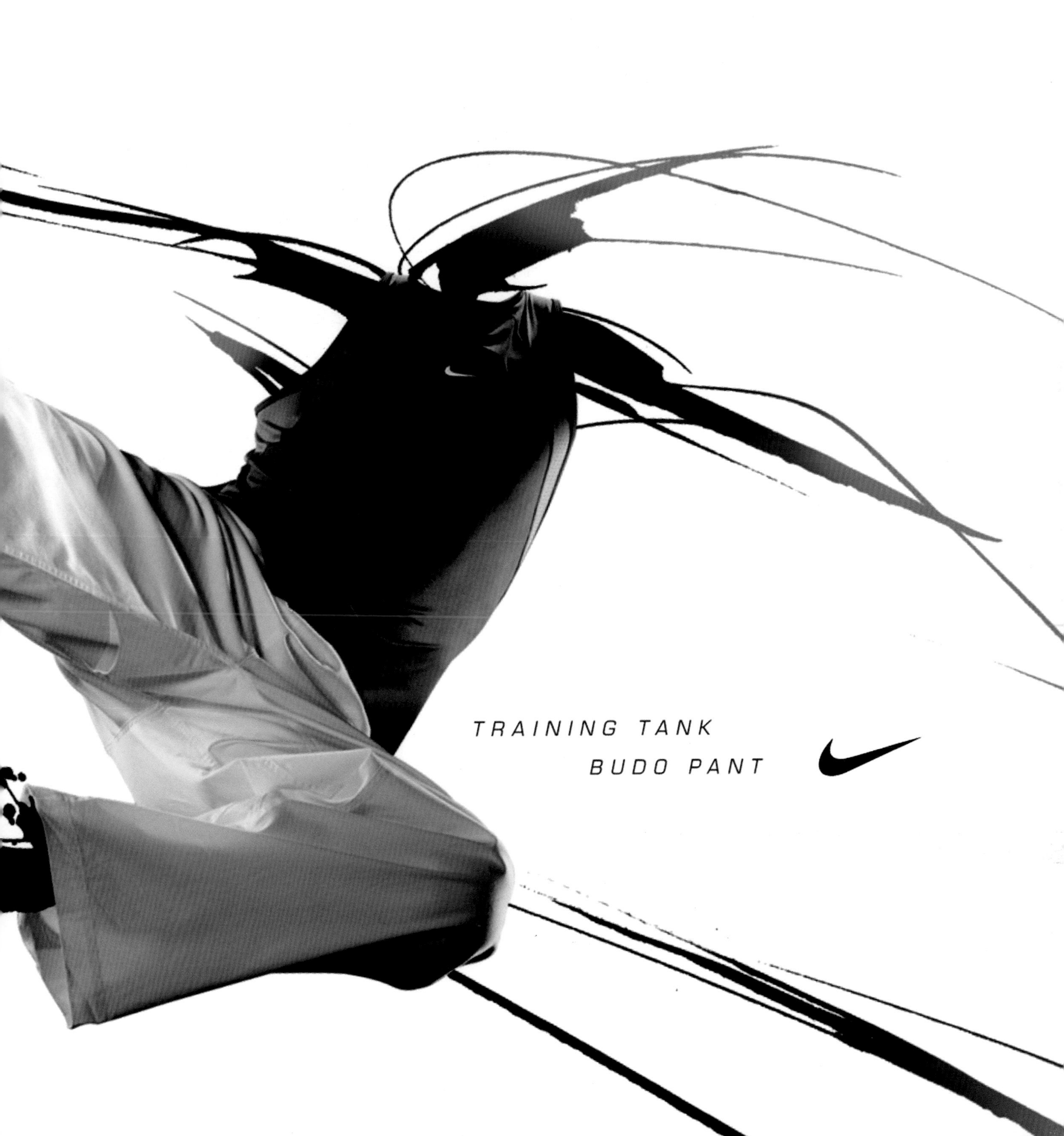
TRAINING TANK
BUDO PANT

24 Puma illustration for Bij magazine (NL)

PUMA

Neiman Marcus

THIS PAGE ›
above: Alexander McQueen, Pool Magazine, (Japan)
below: Neiman Marcus Gallery promotion

OPPOSITE ›
Neiman Marcus Accessory promotion

Woman with Hat I, personal work

 THIS PAGE › Being, personal work OPPOSITE › above: Puritans, personal work below: One, personal work

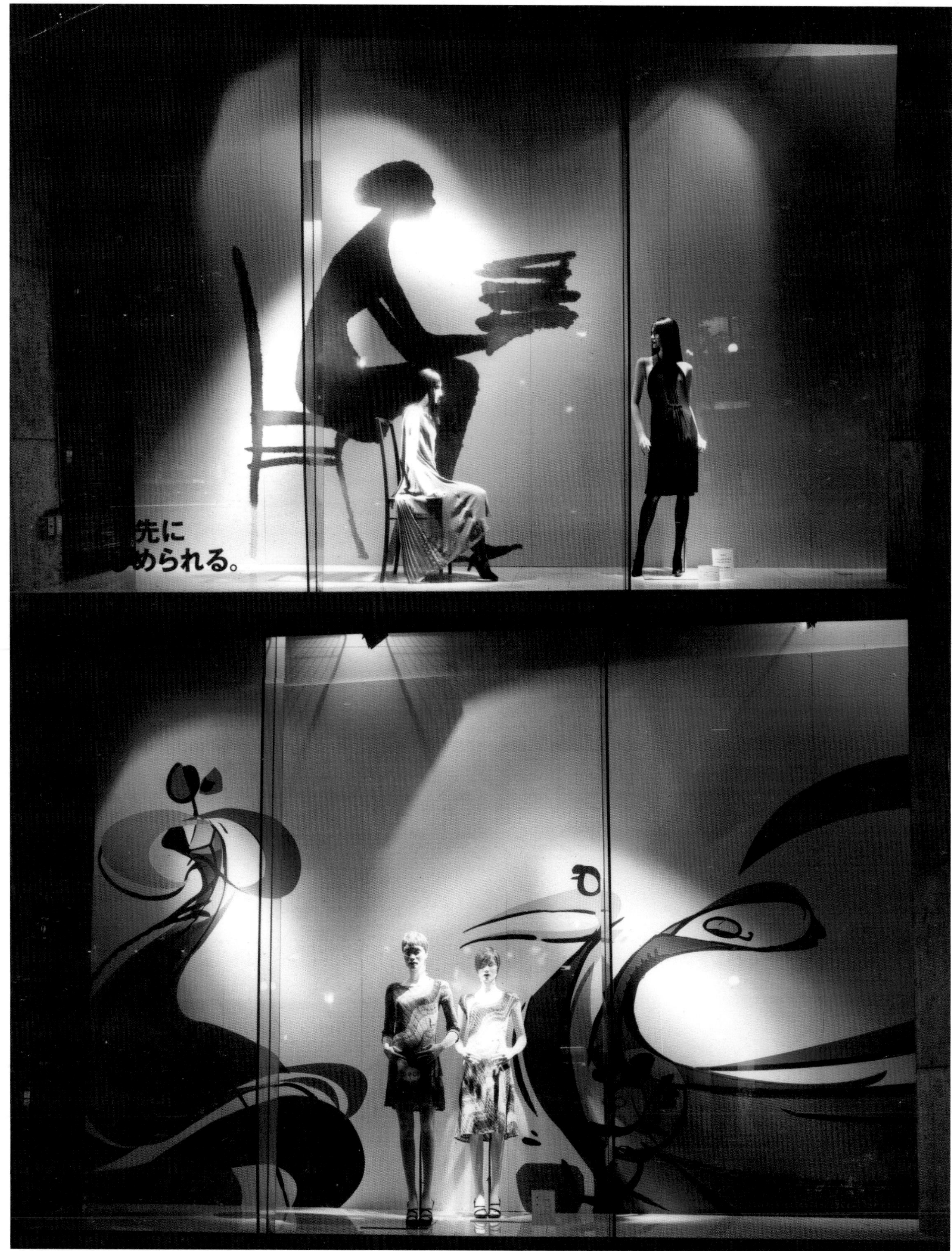

THIS PAGE › above: Window Art - Spring, Seibu Department Stores (Japan) below: Window Art - Fall, Seibu Department Stores (Japan) OPPOSITE › Spring Lady, personal work

blooms, personal work

MCMLXXIV
REC
VOL

NIKE, Mural painting for Nike Art Project
on Elizabeth st. Noli

KENZO MINAMI USA

FLAUNT

Special Fall Fashion Issue

Luxuria Locuples Pecuniosus Aureus

ian somerhalder coldplay marisa tomei thievery corporation

CHARLIZE THERON

$6.95 U.S. $8.95 CANADA

7 25274 93194 1 37

Les Fleurs du Mal
Utility and emotional satisfaction since 1974
XLR8R
+33
© MMIII KENZO MINAMI
Mk-III
Part 2
Chainsaw Massacre in Paris

 THIS PAGE › Eleven, Personal Work OPPOSITE › Addict, for Addict magazine (Amsterdam), Art Direction / Art work by Kenzo Minami, Photo by nagi

aculeus
D
Diana

KUSTAA SAKSI

FINLAND

THIS PAGE › Upper Playground (USA) OPPOSITE › Mate Recordings (UK)

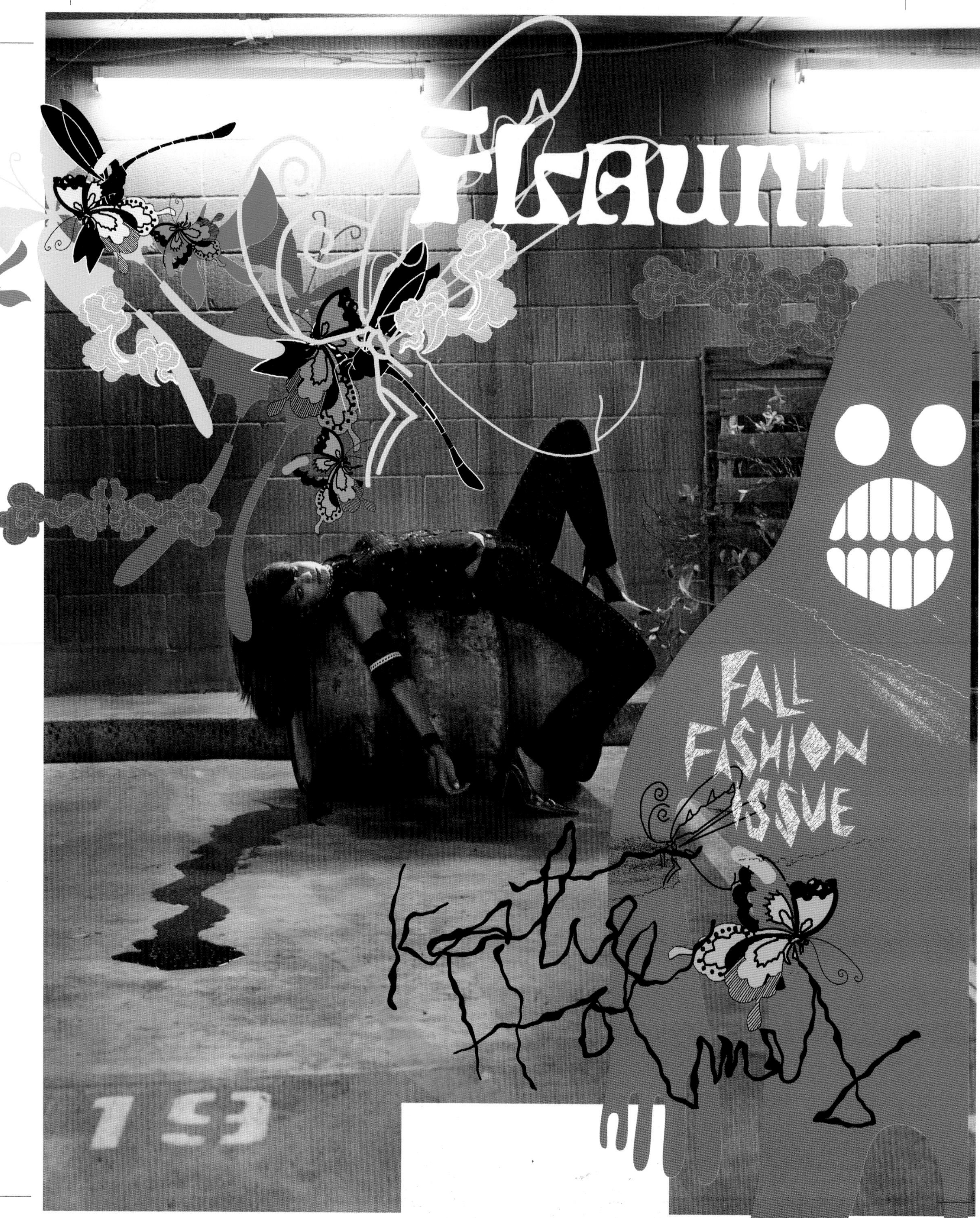

THIS PAGE › Flaunt Magazine (USA) OPPOSITE › Man magazine (The Netherlands)

THIS PAGE & OPPOSITE › Man magazine (The Netherlands)

KangaROO
KangaROO

JEAN-MARIE ANGLES

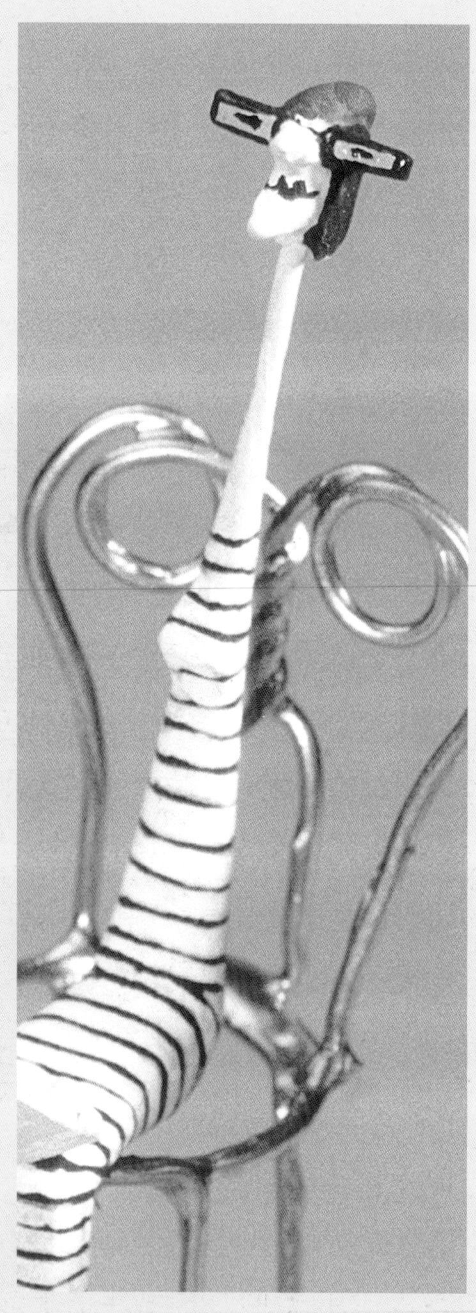

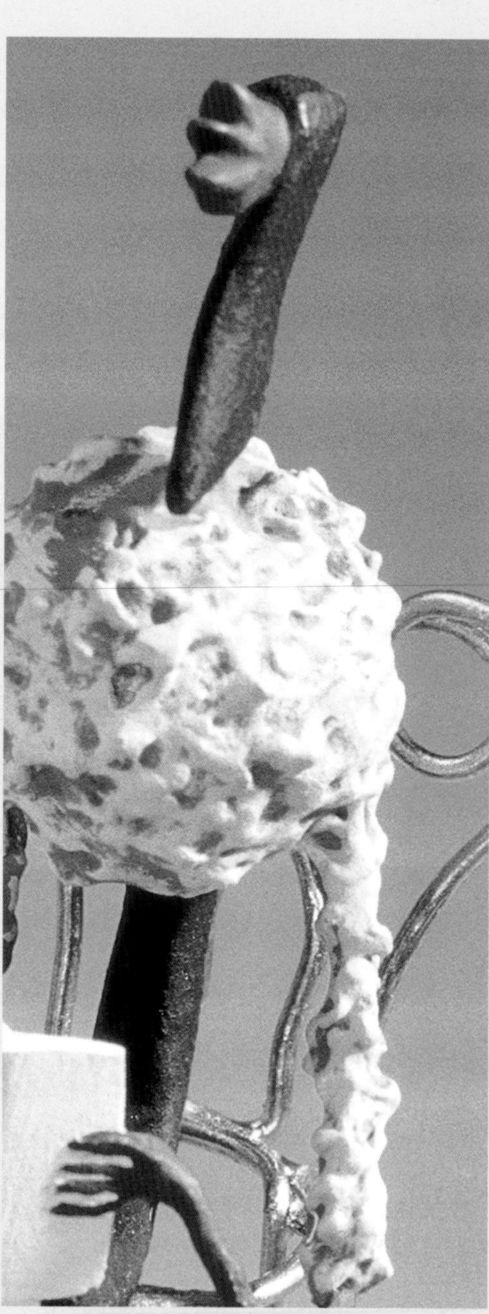

FRANCE

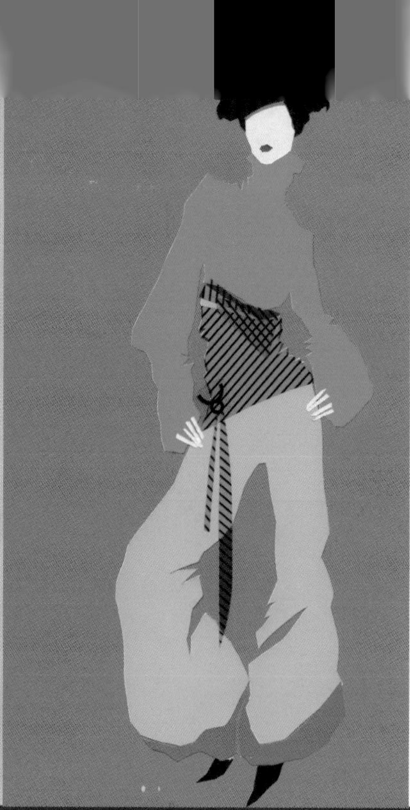

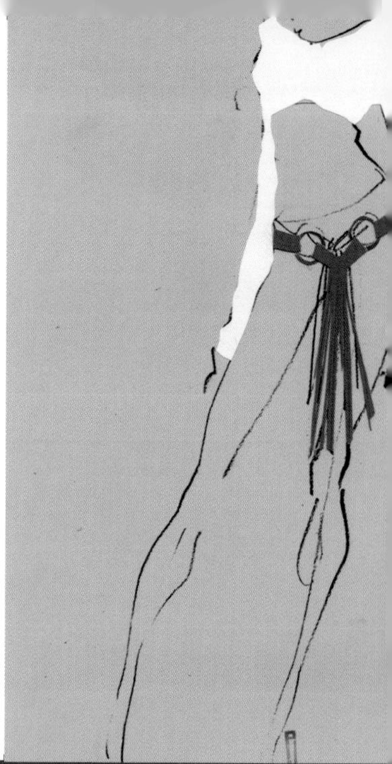

PIERRE-LOUIS MASCIA

FRANCE

THIS PAGE & OPPOSITE › Vogue Pelle

THIS PAGE › Vogue Pelle OPPOSITE › Magnum inc japan

TSUYOSHI HIRANO

JAPAN

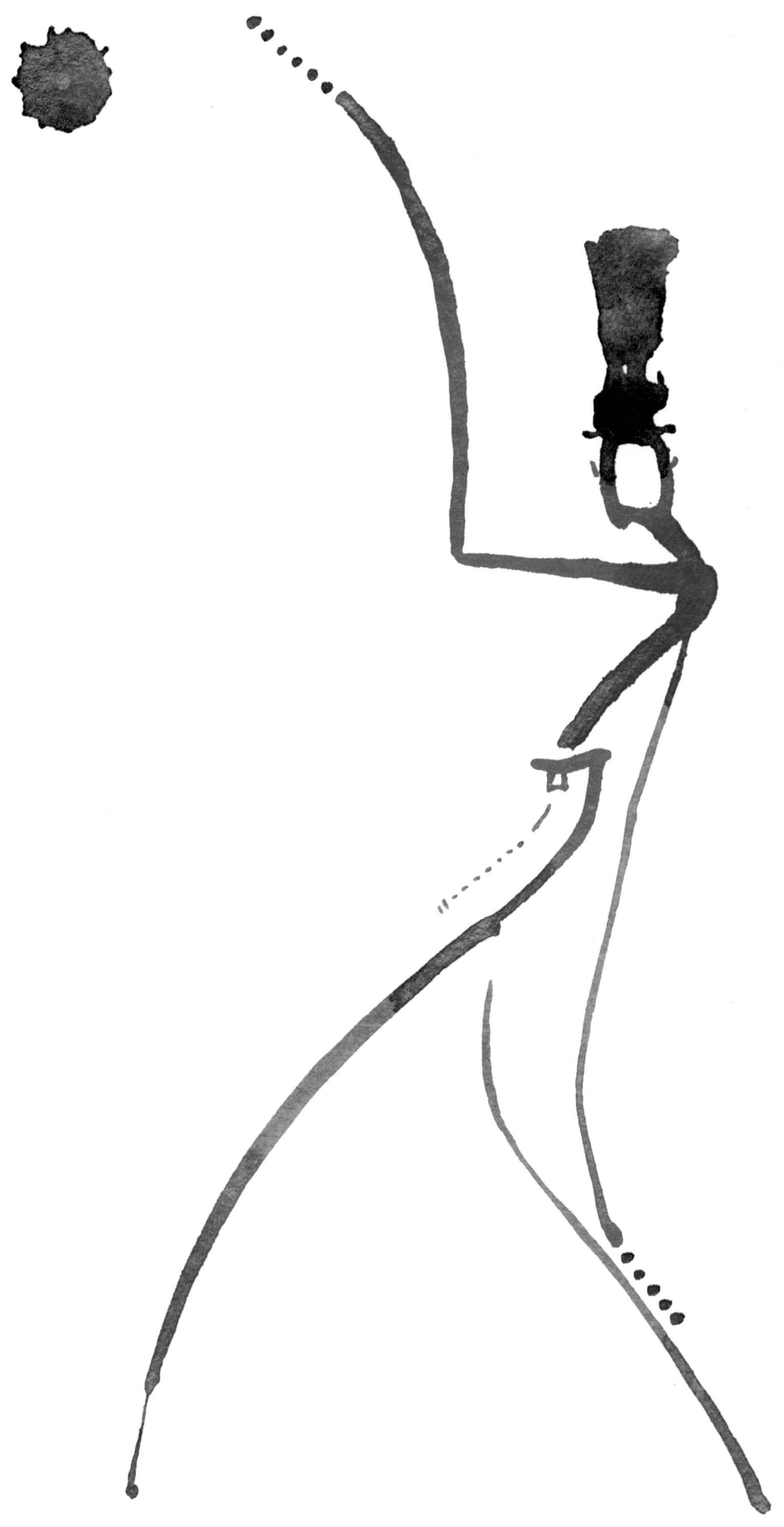
HIRANO.

 THIS PAGE Above › Dossier de Presse,Sacs Happy, CARTIER International Below › left: Magazine GLOSS N°6 (France) right: personal work OPPOSITE › personal work

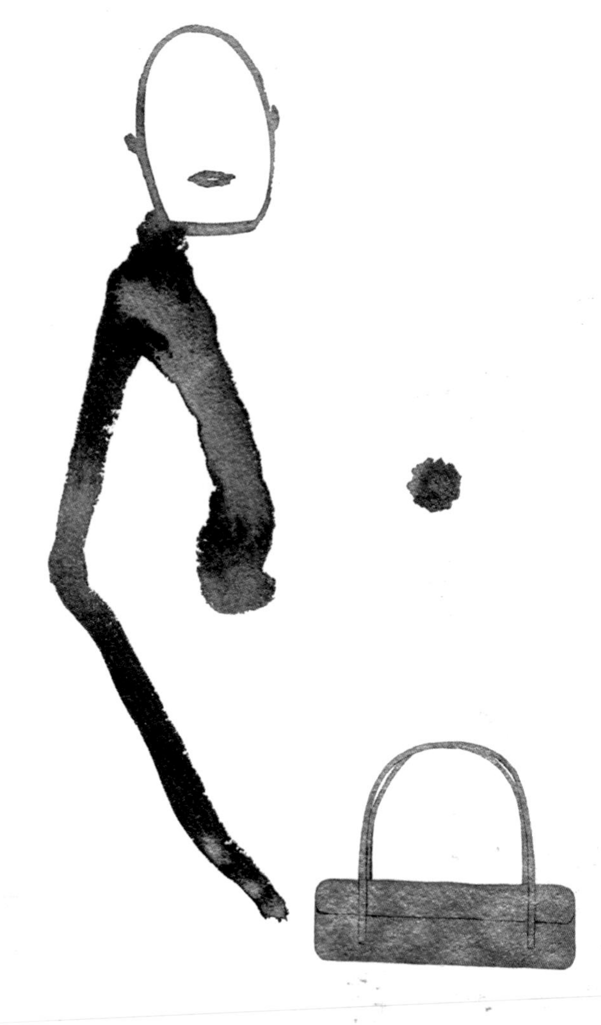

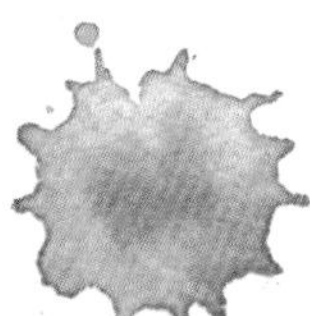

HIRANO.

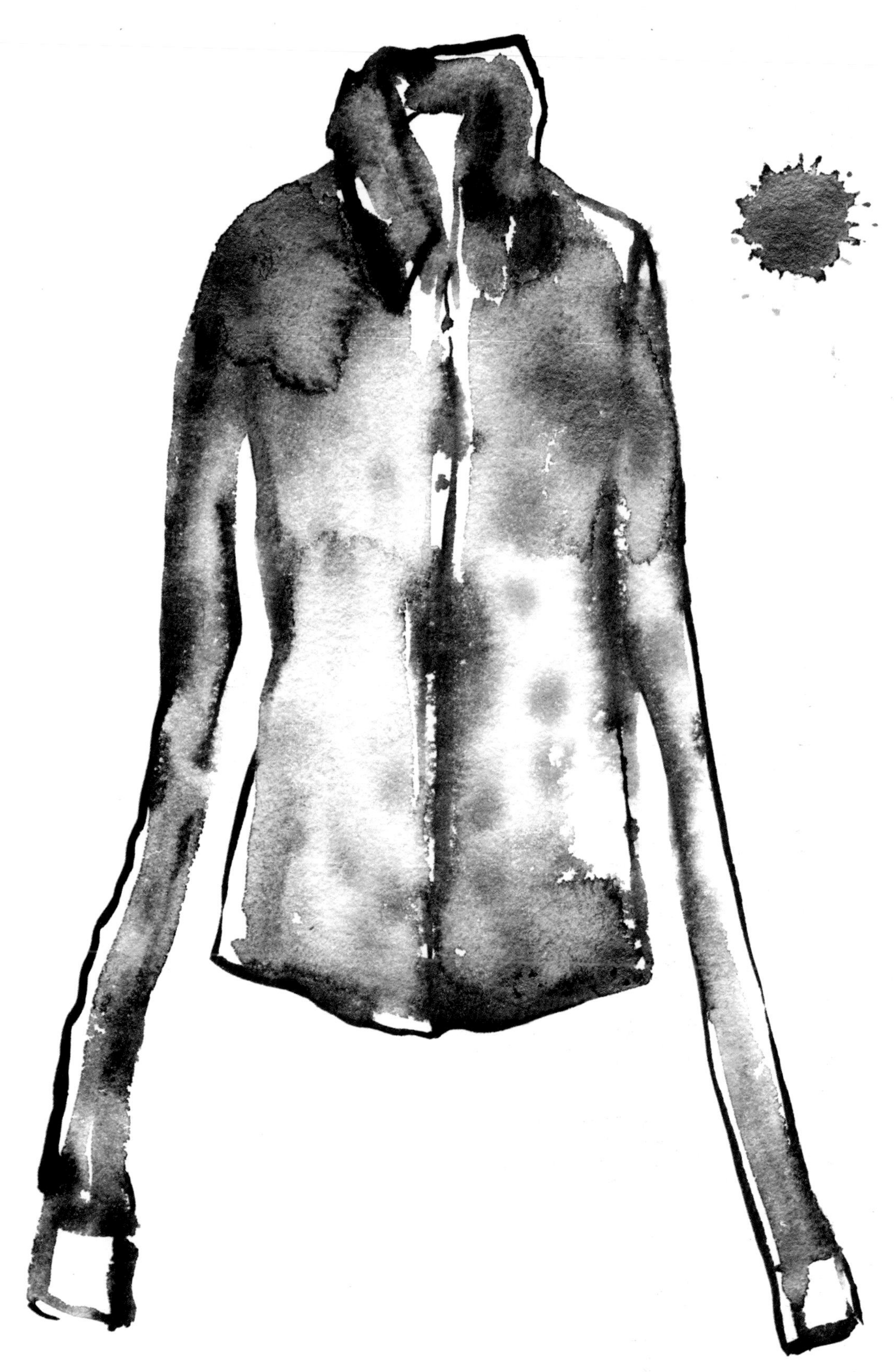
HIRANO.

 THIS PAGE › Badoit bottle, Pro' Deo Agency, Badoit (DANONE). OPPOSITE › Cover Magazine AUDREY (Italy)

HIRANO.

MARY LYNN BLASUTTA

USA

THIS PAGE & OPPOSITE › personal works

THIS PAGE › Libra, Elle Quebec, series of 12 horoscopes for montlhy magazine OPPOSITE › Nordstrom Girl, Nordstrom Stores,opening invitation

mary lynn blasutta

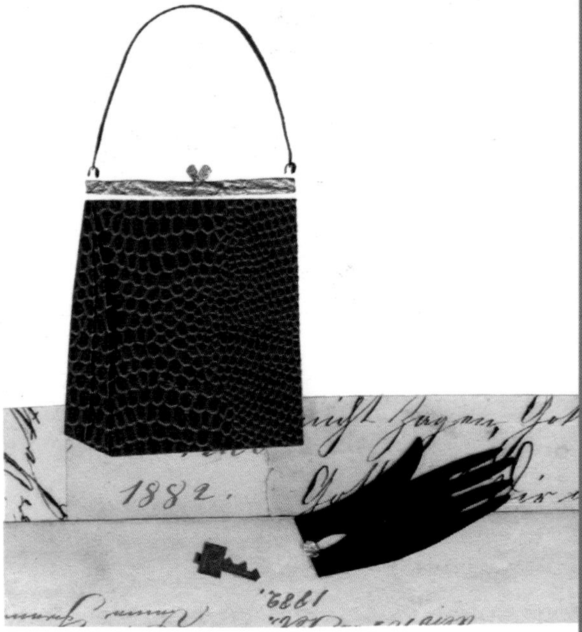

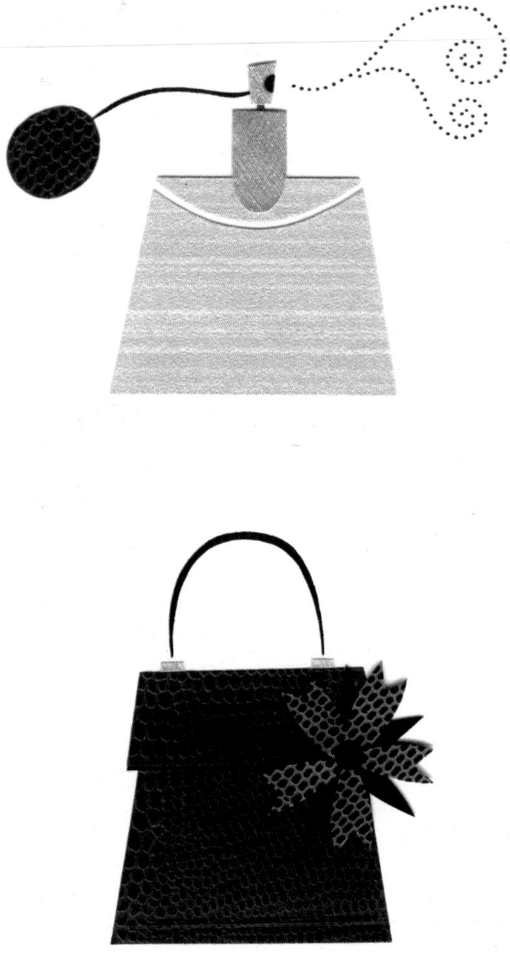

ABOVE › left: personal work › right: Lady dinning w/dog. Victoria Magazine BELOW › left: Perfume & pocketbook, In Style, promotional campaign › right: Elevator girl Saks Fifth Avenue In-store display series of five

upclose

they love to watch

Wanna know which Hollywood star is totally absorbed by SpongeBob SquarePants? *We've got your broadcast news*

Sarah Jessica Parker may be dealing with the demands of new motherhood, but she still can't bear to miss an episode of *The Osbournes*. And with Tivo—a digital video recorder that can store up to 80 hours of TV programming and even selects and records shows based on users' viewing habits—she doesn't have to. "Breast-feeding is an around-the-clock deal," explains Parker. "During those very lonely early-morning hours, I watch what I've Tivo'd [yes, it has become a verb]: *Frontline, The Amazing Race, Curb Your Enthusiasm, 60 Minutes, The Osbournes* and anything with Spencer Tracy." (What, no reruns of *Square Pegs*?) Parker's not alone in front of the small screen—Ben Affleck, Heather Locklear, Samuel L. Jackson, Sarah Michelle Gellar and Britney Spears all use the gadget to catch up on their colleagues. Or even to indulge in a little déjà viewing: "I feel weird about it, but I've Tivo'd myself," says Garcelle Beauvais-Nilon. "I got tons of *Jamie Foxx* shows and the times I was on *Arli$$*." But even stars who watch the old-fashioned way can't get enough tube time. Flip through the following pages to see what makes Hollywood's must-see-TV list. —**Elyssa Lee**

Ben Affleck

Sarah Jessica Parker

IN STYLE APRIL 2003 **285**

HOROSCOPE

OCTOBRE 2003

Balance

Du 23 juillet au 23 août

Parce que la vie vous a donné le goût du dépassement et une grande exigence envers vous-même et les autres, la réussite vous sourit à pleines dents. Votre nature impérieuse ne se satisfait pas de la «bonne moyenne» et encore moins de la médiocrité. Il vous faut du prestige, du luxe et de l'or. Avouez que ces derniers temps, Jupiter vous a réservé la part du... lion. Avec son passage en Vierge, à la fin du mois, il faudra cependant vous attendre à des moments moins éclatants. Mais ce que vous aurez l'impression de perdre en faste, vous le

VIERGE

Du 24 août au 23 sept.

Pas de doute, c'est votre mois! Portée par un délicieux amas planétaire dans votre signe, vous vous sentirez pousser des ailes. Vous éprouverez le désir soudain de vivre plus intensément, de prendre des risques. Et, surtout, de vous lancer dans l'inconnu sans vous soucier de ce que les autres pensent, même tout bas. Cette envie d'indépendance conquérante étant nouvelle, il n'est pas étonnant que vous vous sentiez quelque peu déstabilisée. Mais pas de panique: cette fin d'été n'annonce que du bon.

BALANCE

Du 24 sept. au 23 oct.

Avec Mercure qui fait des siennes, ce n'est pas le moment de vous poser trop de questions, surtout en ce qui a trait à vos relations affectives. Vrai, Justine, votre amie de toujours, s'éloigne; Jean-Paul, votre flamme, n'en fait qu'à sa tête. Résultat? Vous sentez monter en vous un vague sentiment de dépendance qui vous étreint autant qu'il vous éteint. Mon conseil: cultivez votre jardin secret, multipliez les sorties en solo, tenez un journal; retrouvez-vous, quoi. Tout vous apparaîtra plus facile.

SCORPION

Du 24 oct. au 22 nov.

Femme sous l'influence de Mars et d'Uranus, je vous envie. À vous le punch, l'énergie et le sens de l'improvisation. À vous encore l'inspiration, l'audace et le génie! Pas une seconde d'ennui, garanti! Ouste, les pensées limitatives, les doutes inutiles, les craintes irraisonnées... Mais bon, n'attendez pas qu'une occasion se présente, imaginez-la et créez-la! «C'est bien joli tout ça, mais si ça tourne mal?» vous demandez-vous in petto. Pas de souci, vous ne courez aucun risque. C'est pas fantastique, ça?

SAGITTAIRE

Du 23 nov. au 21 déc.

Avis aux retardataires et autres adeptes de la procrastination - vous, peut-être? C'est le mois dernier qu'il fallait vous jeter à corps perdu dans un projet ou dans le premier avion. Mais bon, puisque le ciel est clément, il vous invite à profiter des deux premières semaines du mois pour vous remuer le popotin. Après, ne venez pas vous plaindre! D'ici là, profitez-en pour améliorer votre vie côté cœur, sans pour autant viser la perfection à tout prix; cela ne vous mènerait qu'à la frustration. Vu?

ALEX VALLIÈRES

ELLE QUÉBEC 1

oscars a to z

Want to know more Oscar secrets than those Price Waterhouse Coopers accountants? The juicy big-night goss is all right here

BY MONICA CORCORAN

A IS FOR ATTACHES, those black leather Longchamp briefcases carried by a pair of Price Waterhouse Coopers accountants and containing the sealed envelopes that announce the winners. "One year Robin Williams lunged for [the case], saying, 'Let's get this over with!'" recalls PWC accountant Greg Garrison.

B IS FOR BRIBES, some as high as $US5,000 for a pair of prime seats, says Otto Spoerri, who recently retired from the Academy of Motion Picture Arts and Sciences after 23 years of overseeing the invite list and seating plan. Last year two Academy members (there are 5,739) were caught scalping their two tickets for $US10,000. They are no longer members.

C IS FOR CHAMPAGNE AND CAVIAR, not just for consumption, but also as the ingredients in the Champagne Wishes and Caviar Cremes facial at Verabella in Beverly Hills. "Steve Martin thought we were going to have a drink," recalls owner Vera Kantor, who treated the Oscar host to her $US150 specialty last year.

THE NETHERLANDS

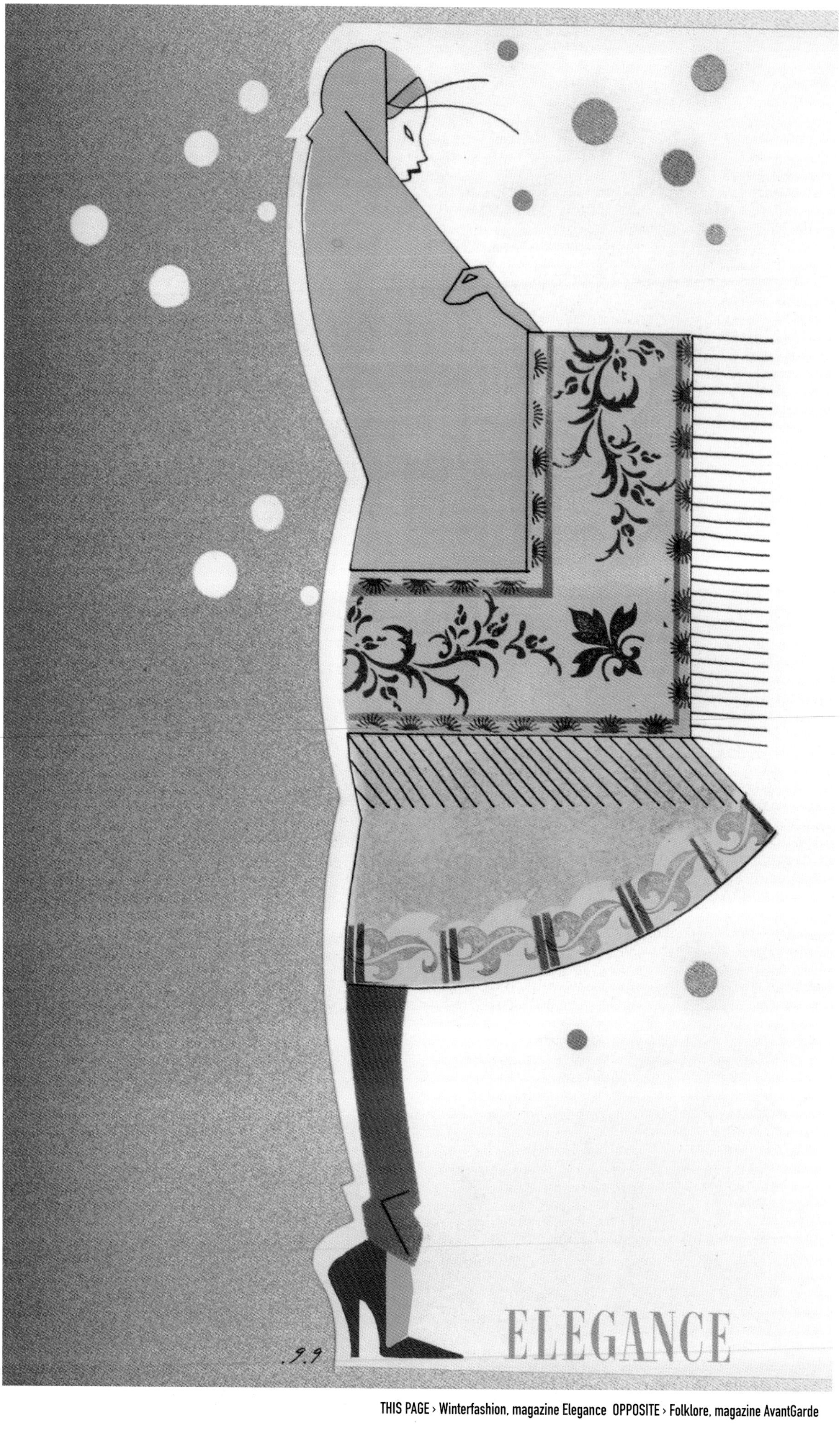

THIS PAGE › Winterfashion, magazine Elegance OPPOSITE › Folklore, magazine AvantGarde

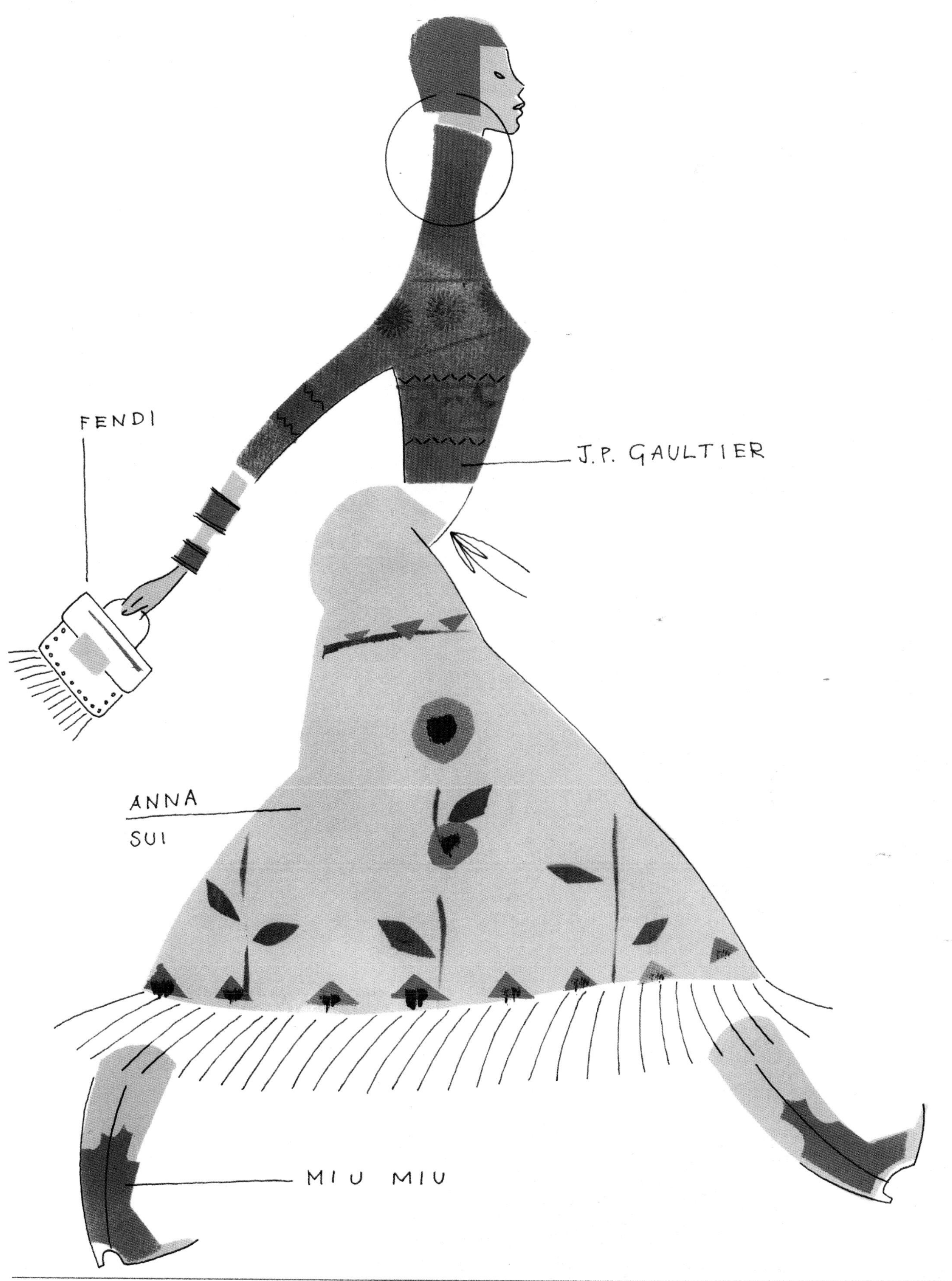

F O L K L O R E

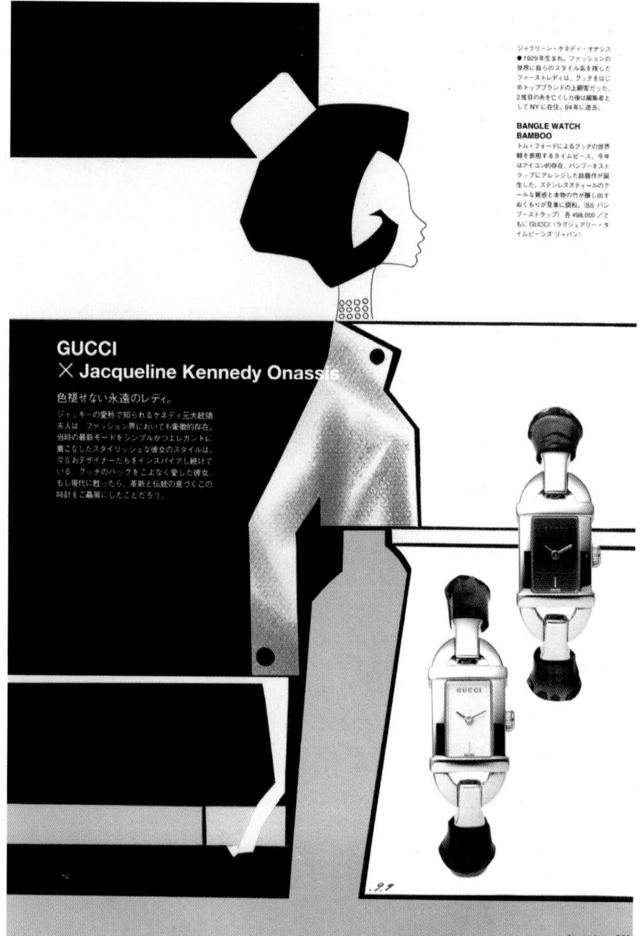

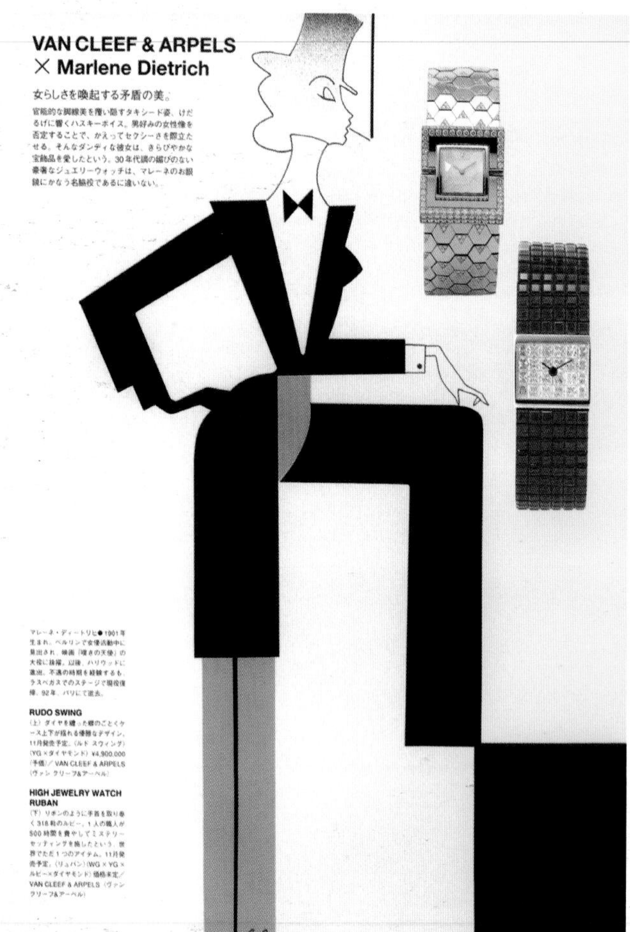

ABOVE left › Twiggy right › jackie BELOW left › Dietrich right › Sophia, VOUGE Japan magazine

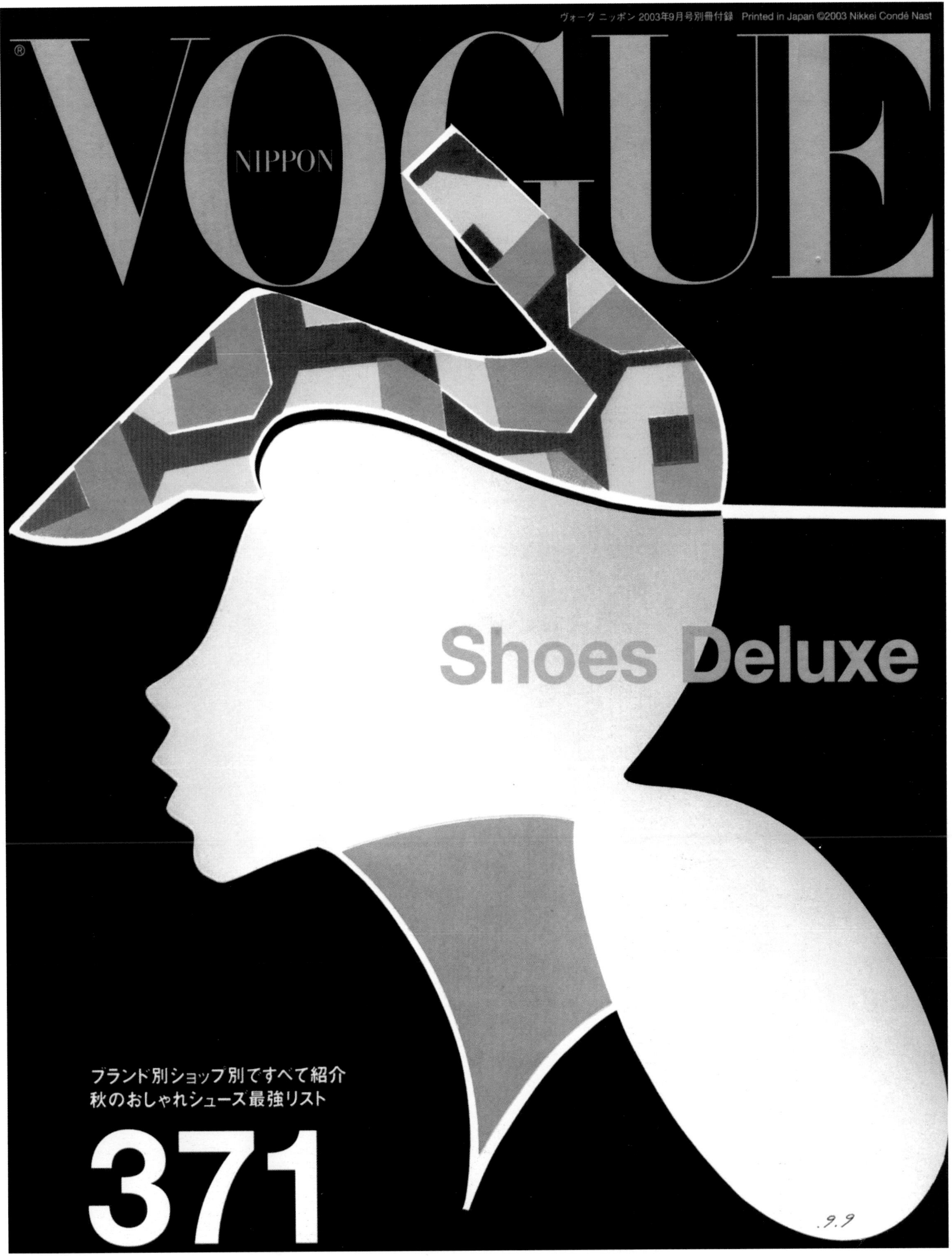

Shoe, VOUGE Japan magazine

Fakefur, departmentstore de Bijenkorf

Viktor & Rolf, DUTCH magazine

Furcoats - magazine Elegance

Relax , Cora Kemperman

Mother and child, Stop AIDS now

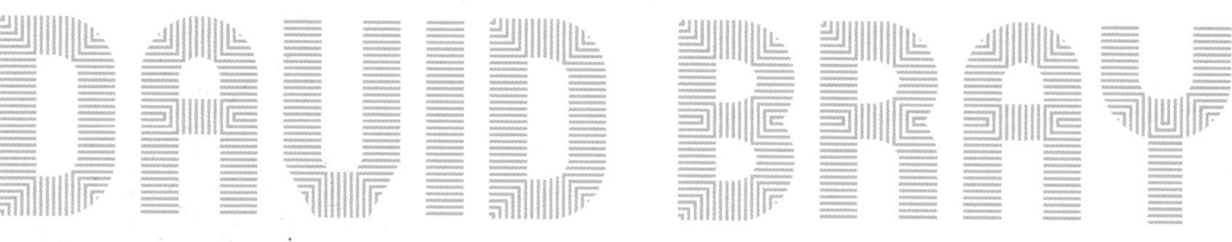
DAVID BRAY
UK

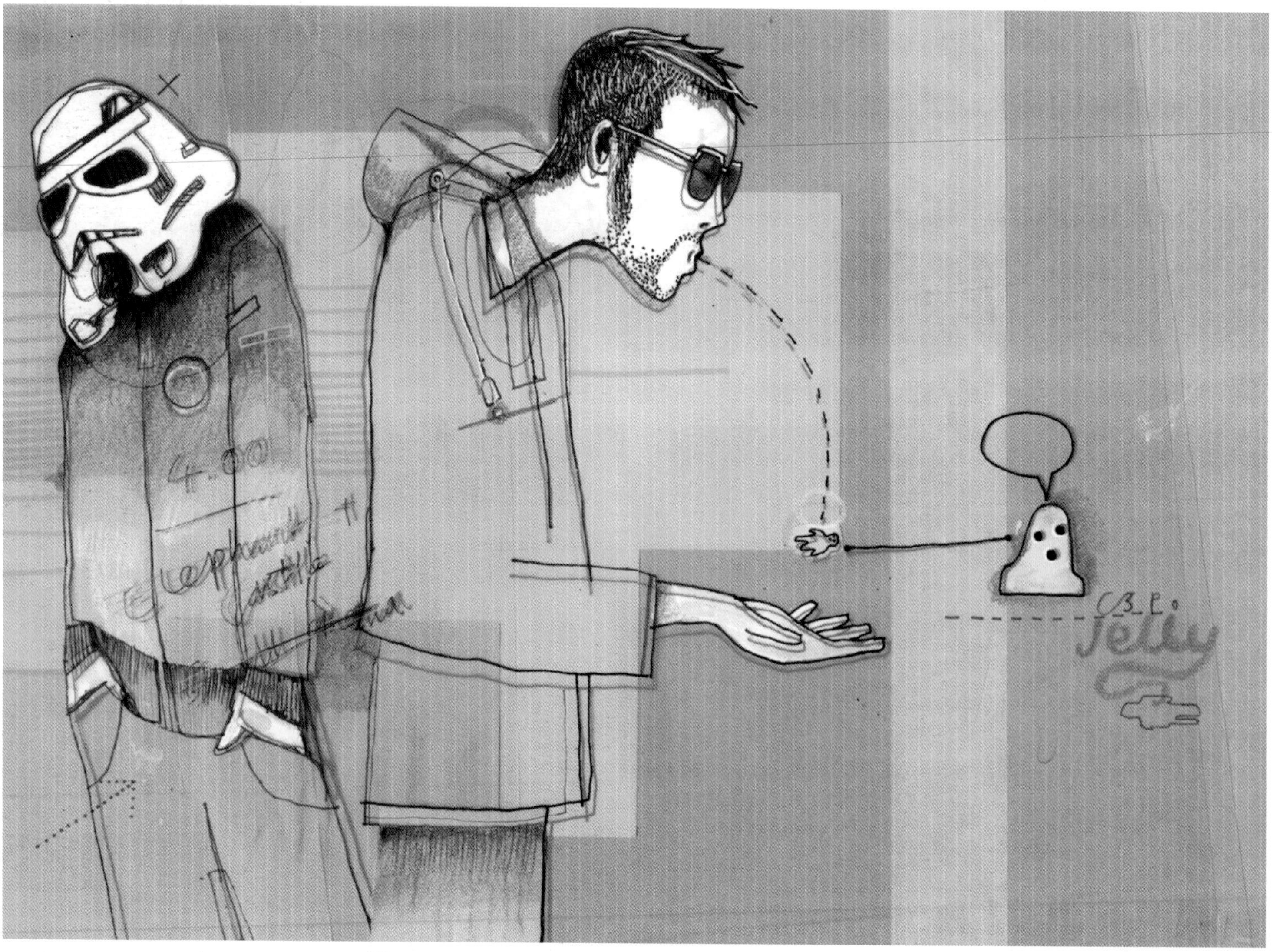

THIS PAGE › 12 people you would like to meet OPPOSITE › jellybean

all the illustrations are personal works

THIS PAGE ABOVE left › rampaccident right › anorak BELOW › siameserabbit OPPOSITE › seagull

STINA PERSSON

SWEDEN

THIS PAGE › shopper, Franco Sarto OPPOSITE › Mc Queen (promotion)

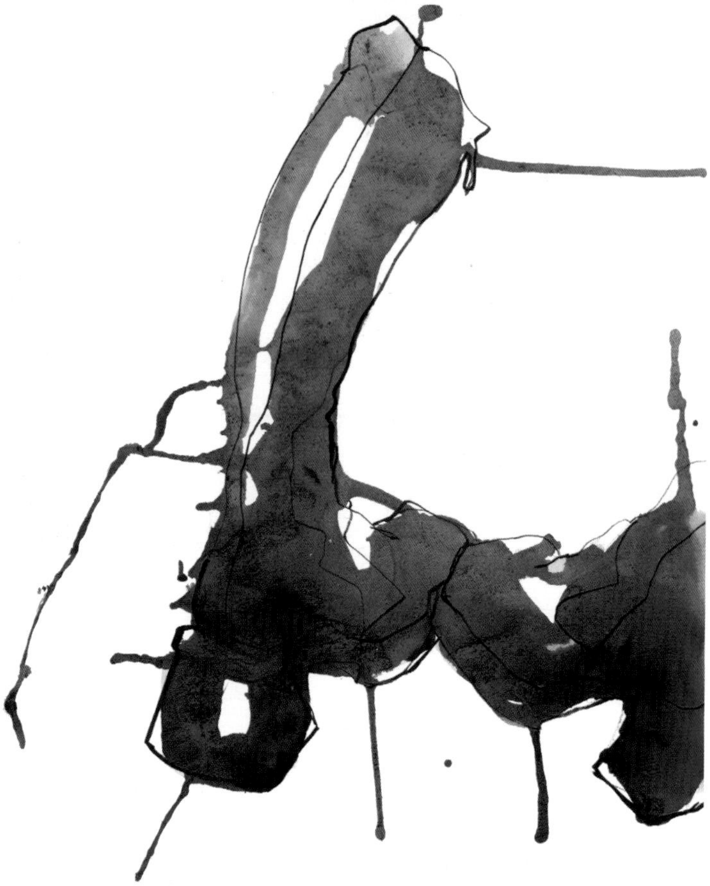

Gucci sandals (promotion)

Boots, CWC gallery

Dandelions (promotion)

Björn Borg Top (black)

Men's underwear, Shell

Björn Borg Top (yellow)

Zodiac feature, ELLE (uk)

LEO
(23 JULY – 23 AUG)

LOVE Let's be honest, you need to be loved and adored the way other people need oxygen. And, lucky you, you *do* seem to get more than the lion's share of affection. But the best way to receive all that loving attention right now is to spread it around. Until 28 August this won't be an issue but, after that, when the love spring dries up and has you almost panic-stricken, practise what comes naturally to Leos: making *others* feel special. The vibe will come back in spades.

SEX It is hot, it is heavy, and it is changing every time you turn around. There are possibilities literally everywhere you turn, which tells you two important things: one, don't plan on shacking up with anyone just yet. Two, you need to work out a little harder than usual since you will be spending so much of the summer and autumn in various states of undress...

MONEY Spending money has never been a problem for you, and from July till the end of August you may actually set a personal record. But sometime between 23 and 28 August, a light goes on in your head, making it very clear to you that if you have some big plans for the coming year, and if those plans involve shifting major amounts of capital, you'd better start saving *now*.

LEO will say it loud with Christian Louboutin's printed calfskin creation, and a hot Moschino frock (left)

VIRGO
(24 AUG – 23 SEPT)

LOVE In July you're spending so much time hanging out with your mates that you develop a crush on one of them. In August you'll be on to someone new – but don't get carried away. By 23 August you'll know if it's for real. September is your best love month, and after 25 October things *really* get cooking!

SEX Casual sex ain't your cup of tea, but with all the changes going on in the rest of your life it's hard to take commitment seriously. You start to get serious about someone in September, but he sends you mixed messages. Let him know he's not the only one with a libido.

MONEY There's no need for you to always get the first round, or dole out cab fare to cash-poor friends every time you're out. It's hard for you to say no, but you must if you're going to afford that new autumn wardrobe. After 16 September, you'll get a raise or new source of income, and around 9 October it gets even better!

VIRGO will be sitting pretty with a chic printed calfskin bag by Salvatore Ferragamo, and in neat, neat, neat Hermès (right)

96 ELLE

LIBRA
(24 SEPT – 23 OCT)

LOVE They say guys think about sex every five minutes, but Libra girls think of romance at least that often. These days, however, it's probably down to twice an hour, thanks to your current workload. Naturally, you have your eye on the hottest guy in the office – but watch your step in September. There'll be a big change in your love life around 9 October, coming completely out of the blue.

SEX If you're not having the multiple orgasms you're accustomed to, don't blame him. Maybe you don't have the energy you need for such Olympic-level activity. Try leaving the office at a reasonable hour for starters. He may act like he's losing interest, but by 1 October you'll realise he isn't. Plan a very special night in on 9 November. He'll never stray again.

MONEY You hate to think about it in the summer, but by the end of August reality catches up with you in the form of credit-card statements, and it's obvious you need to make sweeping economic reforms. Look out for ways to cut right back in September, and by late October you'll be back in the black – black Prada, that is.

LIBRA will feel just swellegant with Celine's printed calfskin boogie bag, and flirty Ungaro (left)

SCORPIO
(24 OCT – 22 NOV)

LOVE You've made a summer resolution to spice up your love life – but you're more interested in a buffet than a meal on a plate. The good news is there are plenty of luscious delicacies to choose from (the difficulty will be getting their names straight). On 10 October you're such a man magnet that friends are hanging around just to pick at your leftovers.

SEX There's 'wild and exciting' to the general populace, and there's 'wild and exciting' to a Scorpio on the prowl. You may find yourself exploring things that even *you* haven't got into before. You won't be able to control all the variables and that may freak you out from 29 July to 27 September. On a serious note, do make sure you have reliable protection. 9 November is a big day.

MONEY You're shrewd about finances, but you like to keep your money situation private. A chance to earn some cash with a partner after 28 August may force you to open up a little. This is worth taking a chance on, but don't expect instant results. However, a big eclipse in your money house on 23 November will bring six months of exciting opportunities. ➤

SCORPIO will be sex-bomb central with Jil Sander's leather shoulder bag, and in a come-hither number by Tom Ford for YSL Rive Gauche (right)

Flowers. 2KT shirt

Spring Issue, Volvo

Zodiac, ELLE (uk)

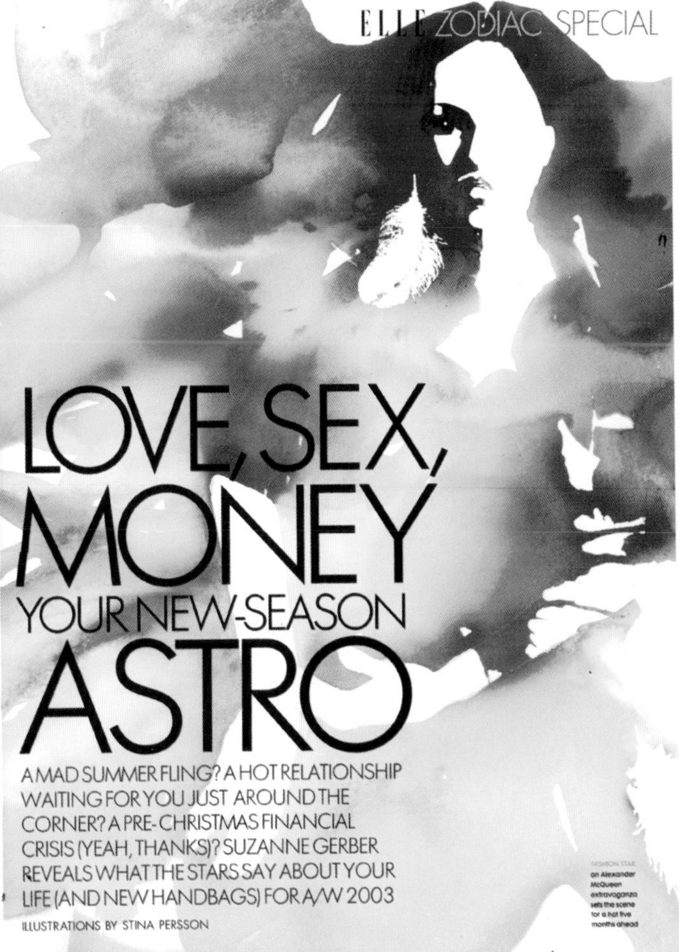

ELLE ZODIAC SPECIAL

LOVE, SEX, MONEY

YOUR NEW-SEASON ASTRO

A MAD SUMMER FLING? A HOT RELATIONSHIP WAITING FOR YOU JUST AROUND THE CORNER? A PRE-CHRISTMAS FINANCIAL CRISIS (YEAH, THANKS)? SUZANNE GERBER REVEALS WHAT THE STARS SAY ABOUT YOUR LIFE (AND NEW HANDBAGS) FOR A/W 2003

ILLUSTRATIONS BY STINA PERSSON

an Alexander McQueen extravaganza sets the scene for a hot five months ahead

Dating, ELLE (uk)

ELLE DATING

2004 YOUR NEW DATING RULES

Fabulous and single – what's up, girlfriend? Danielle Hine has 10 New Year's resolutions to spruce up your dating techniques…

ILLUSTRATION BY STINA PERSSON

1 SAVOUR BEING SINGLE

OK, 'fess up – are you a bit too intense about the dating game? Well, desperation is about as attractive as a pus-filled pimple; just as sitting at home on your butt moping will merely give you saddlebag thighs. To lighten the mood, why not turn the whole thing into a game by playing Dare when you're out with your friends? Each girl gets given a flirting mode – one makes coy eye contact with her favourite totty (provided she's not short-sighted); another tries smiling sexily at the guys she fancies (NB: this does not mean gurning like a loon), and the rest do the making-conversation-with-a-sexy-stranger routine. By turning your night out into a frivolous game (with the champion winning a bottle of champagne), you'll not only find out the approach that works best, but have a laugh doing so. ➤

Hermes, Io Donna Magazine (Italy)

Alviero Martini, Io Donna Magazine (Italy)

LEFT › top: Ruby (book cover, japan) – middle: winte issue (volvo) – below: Morocco, Res magazine – RIGHT: Blue, Arigatt (japan)

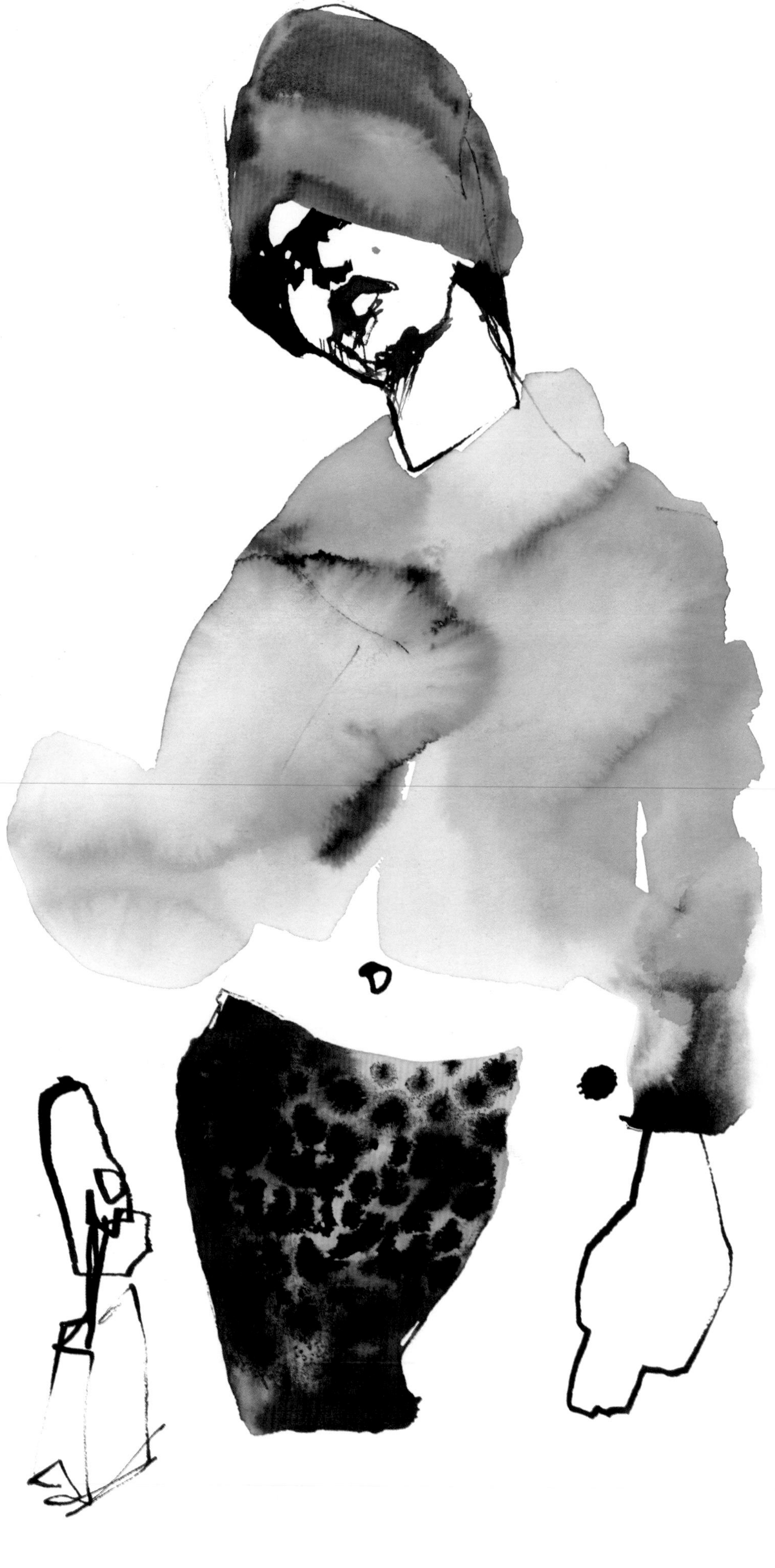

アーティストハウス

Necklace, ELLE (uk)

MAXIME TOURATIER

FRANCE

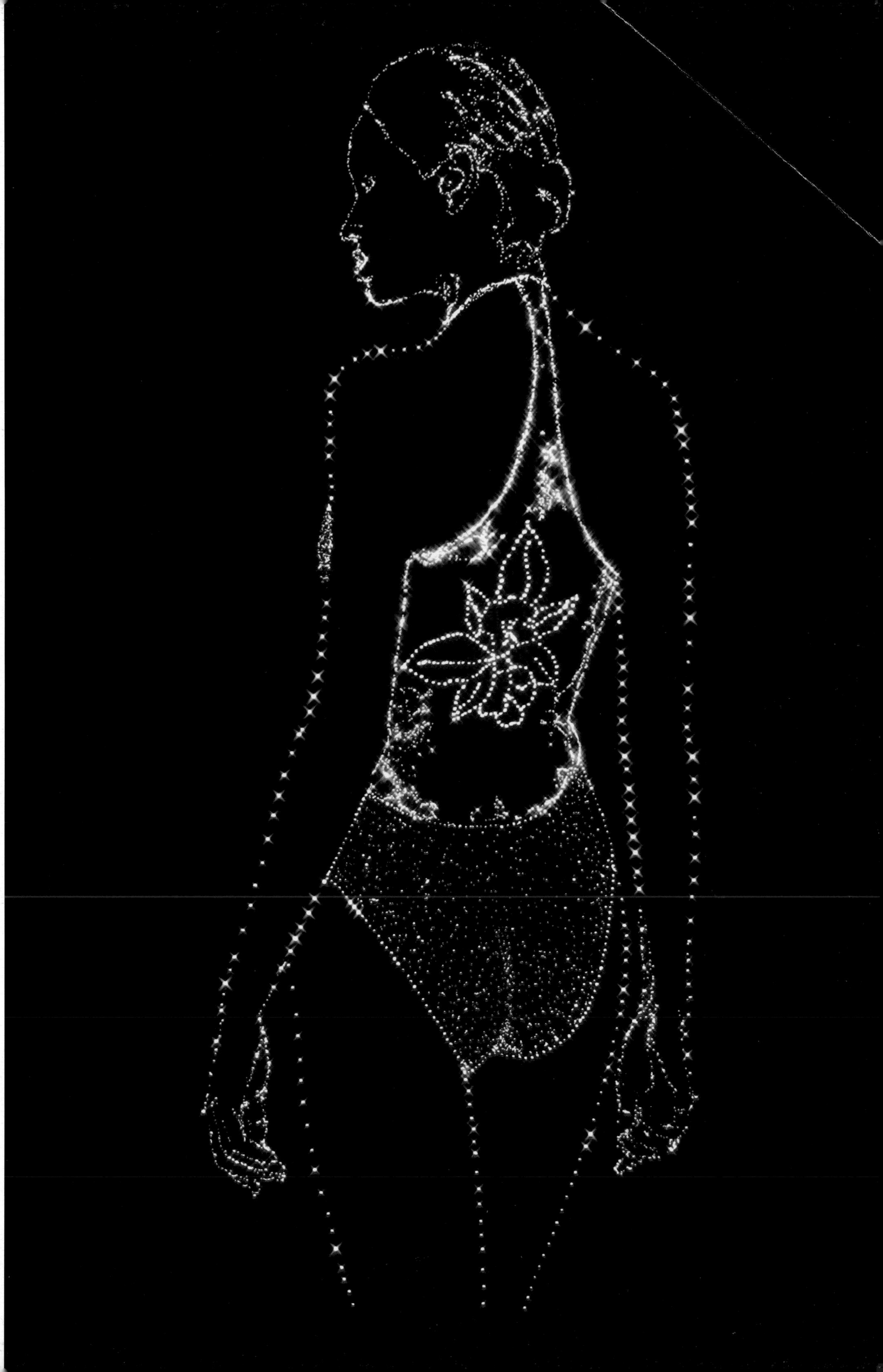

ABOVE LEFT › MOTOROLA, Magazine CLOSS N° 5 (France) RIGHT › DIOR, Magazine CLOSS N° 5 (France) BELOW › COQUELIC, personal work

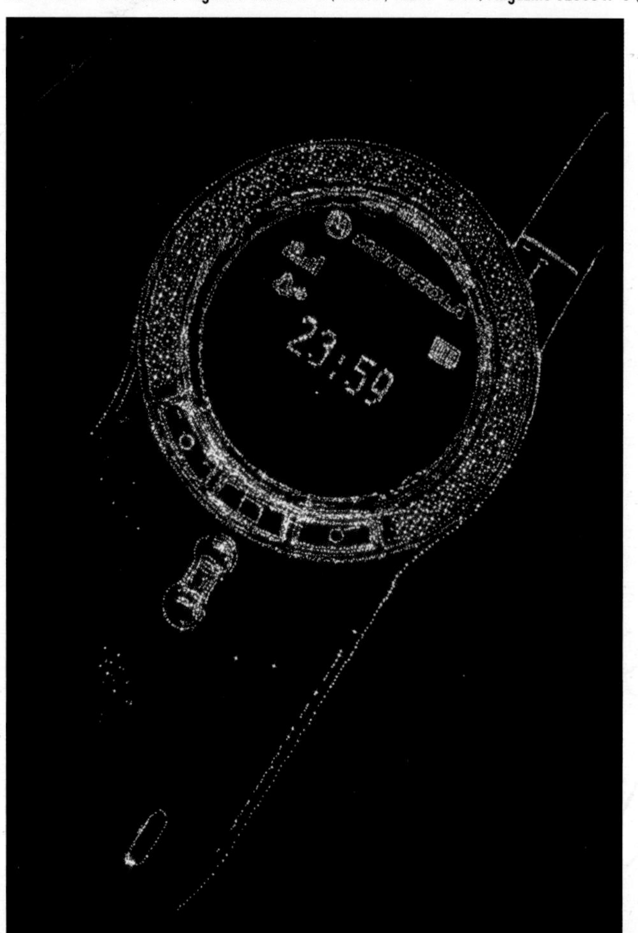

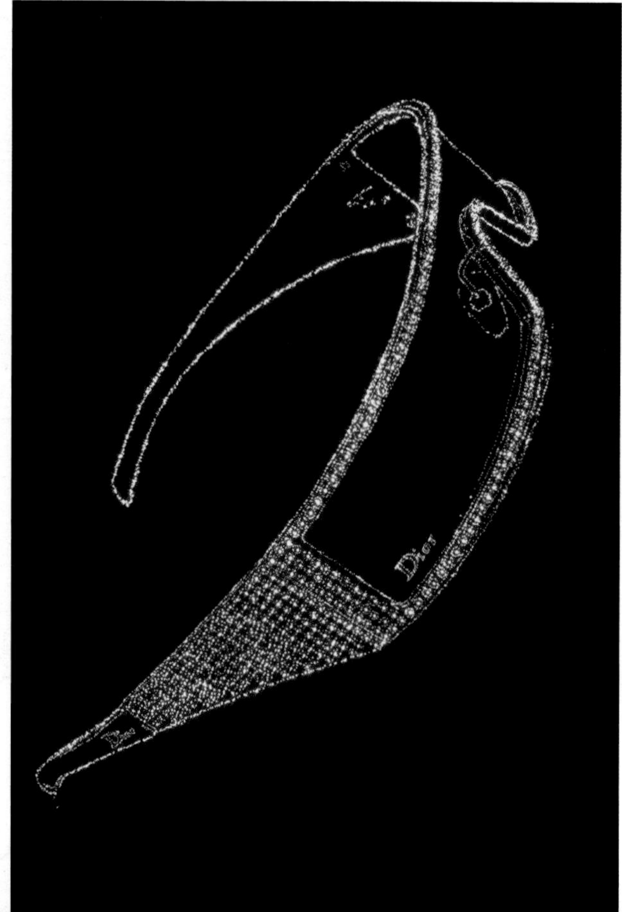

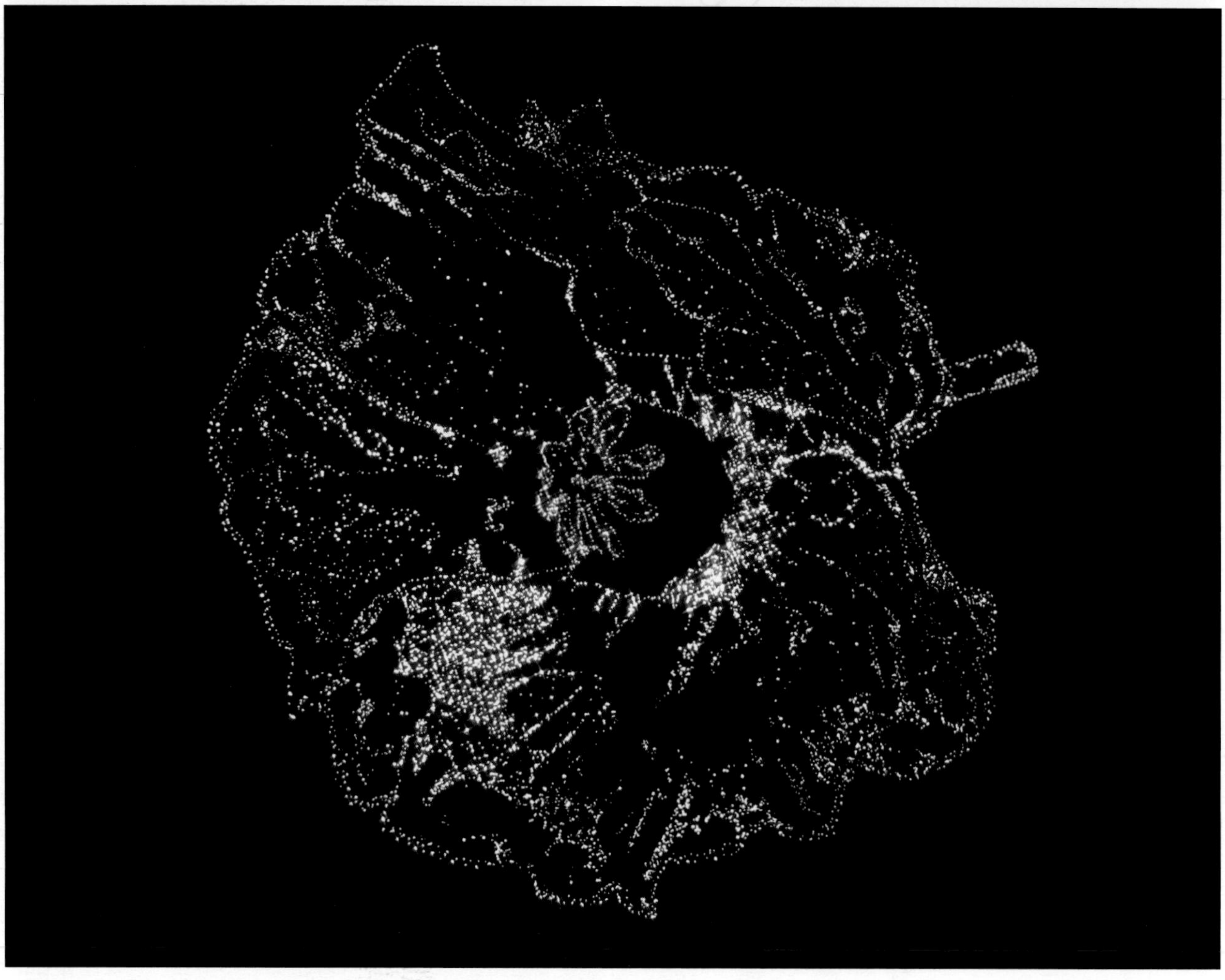

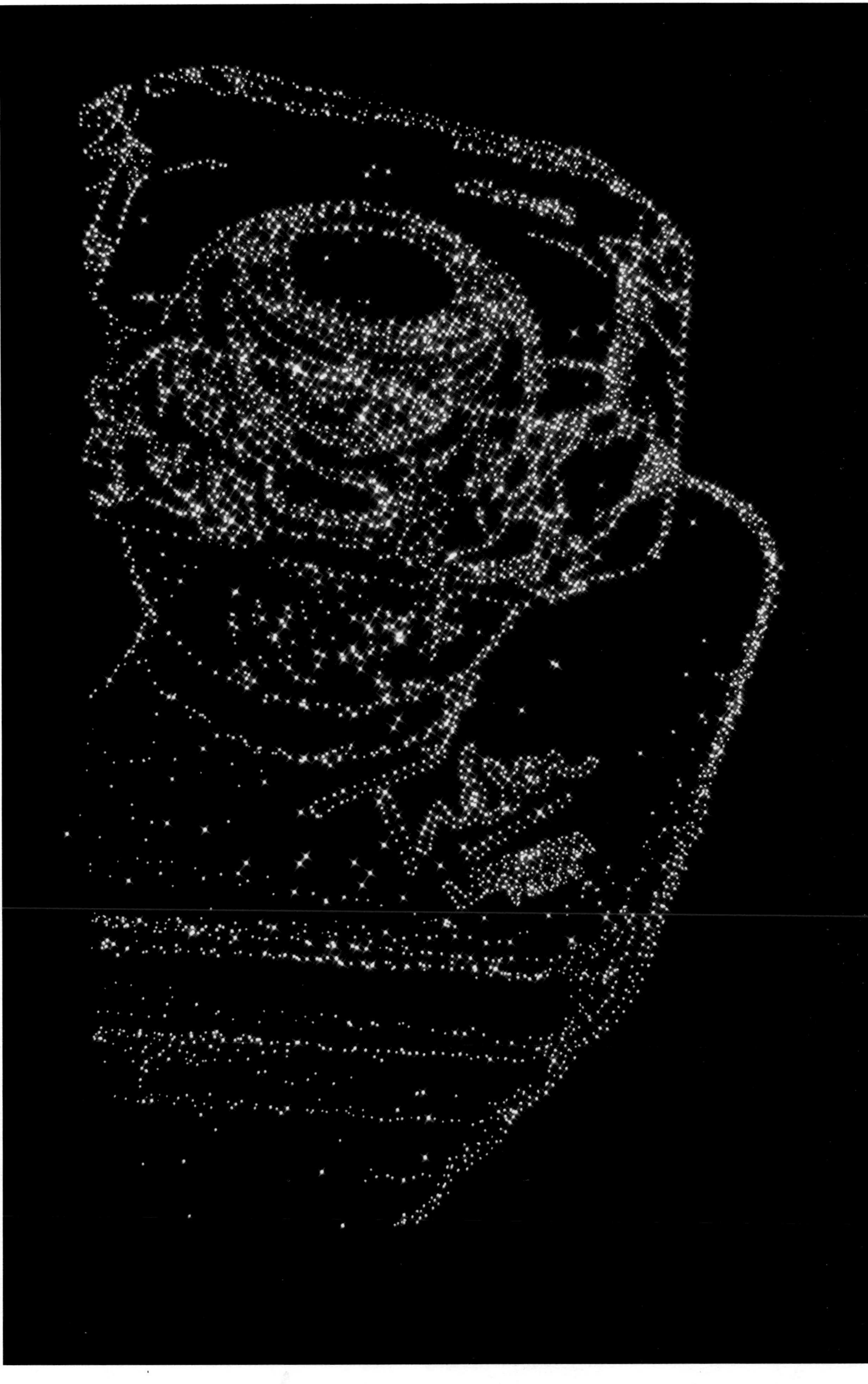

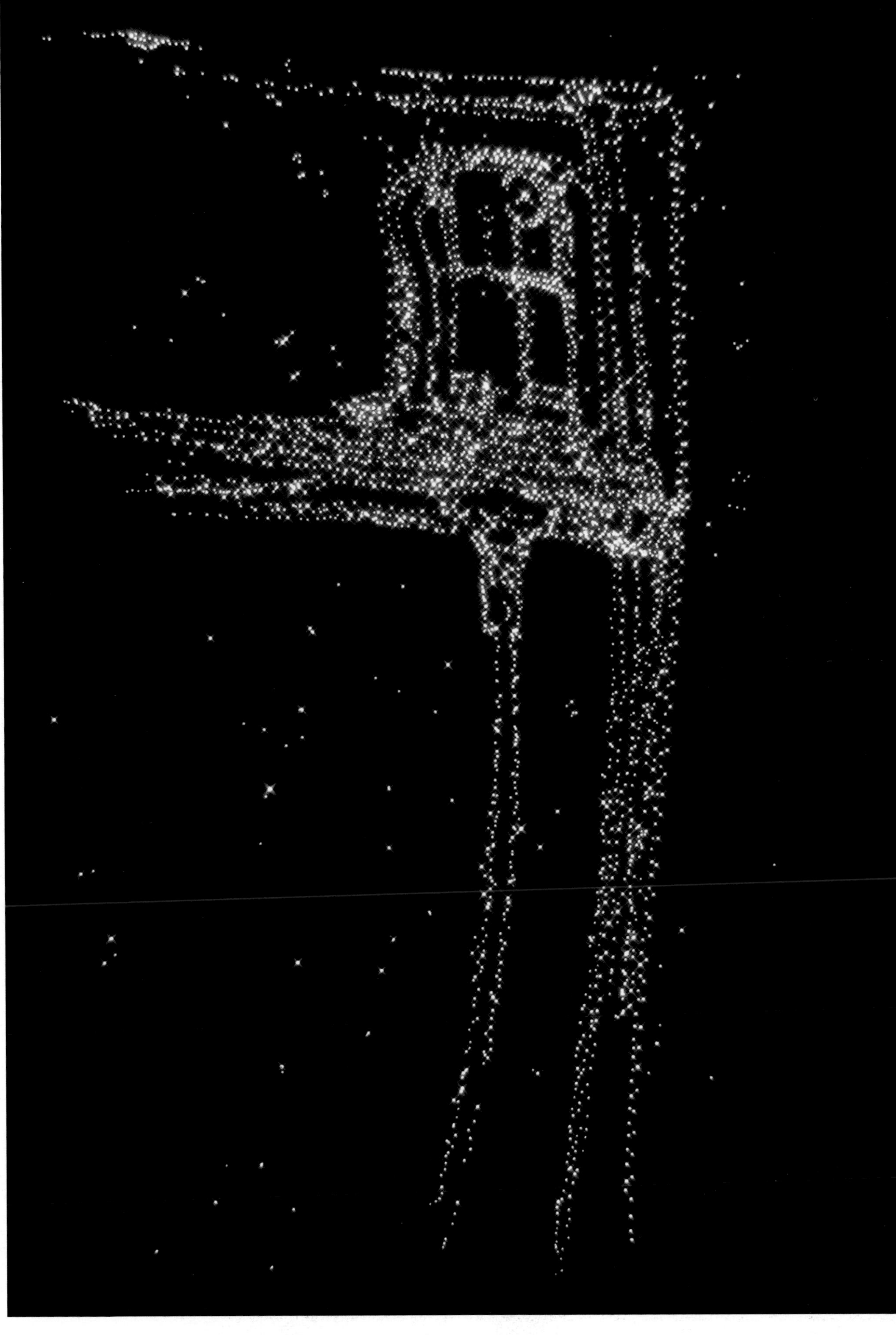

JACQUELINE WHITE

UK

THIS PAGE › collection 01, outfit 4 OPPOSITE › collection 01, outfit

all the illustrations are prsonal works

 ABOVE left › pin right › flamingo & lace BELOW left › cake right › seamstress

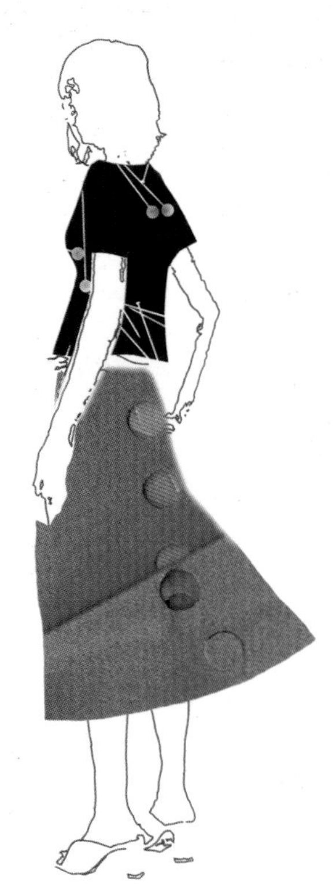

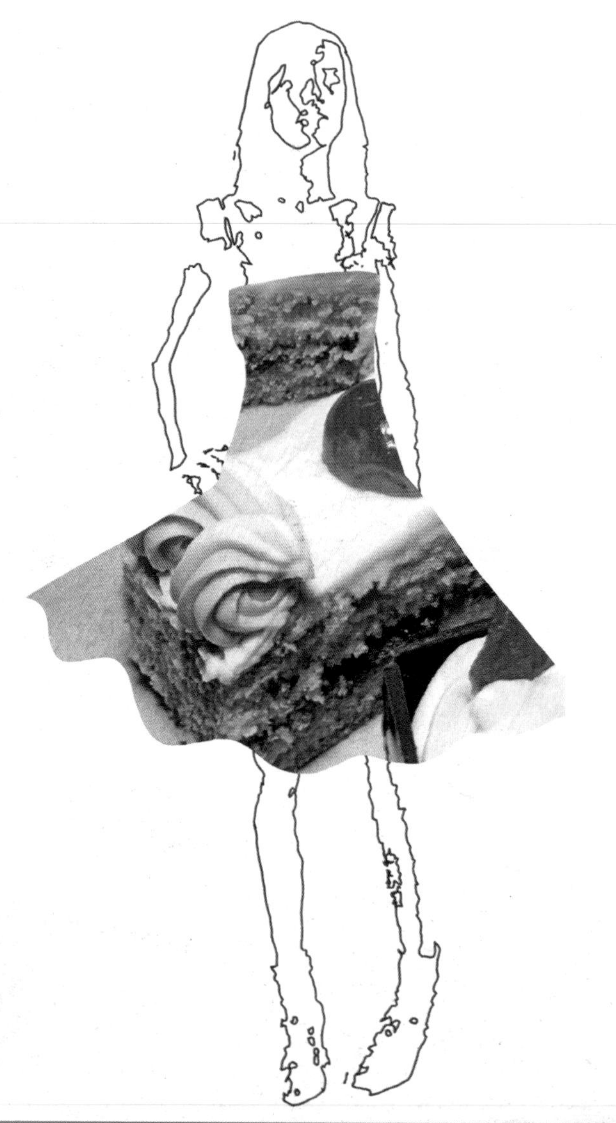

THIS PAGE › Auréus (France) OPPOSITE › Time magazine (USA)

ROBERT WAGT

THE NETHERLANDS

left › Chipie Agency: Anapurna right › KA COVER, Ford, Young & Rubicam (Fr)

Bethesda Row Agency, Good Dog Creative (USA)

DU 7 JANVIER AU 4 FEVRIER
la Part-Dieu
MODE, SHOPPING ET DÉCOUVERTES
partdieu.com
- et encore, j'ai fait hyyyypèèer gaffe
soldes

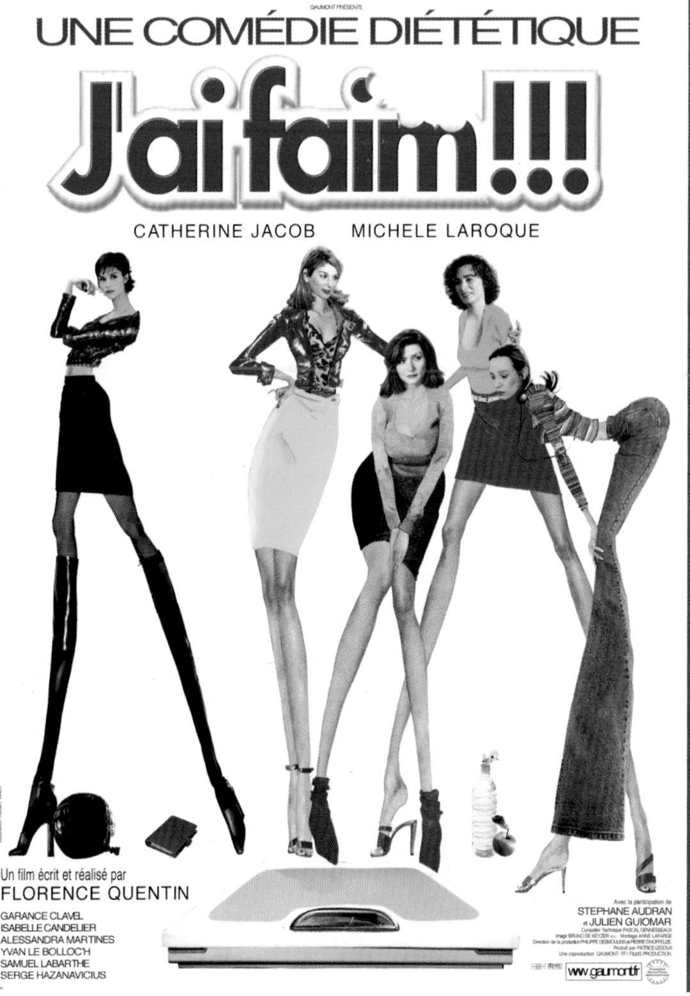
GAUMONT PRÉSENTE
UNE COMÉDIE DIÉTÉTIQUE
J'ai faim!!!
CATHERINE JACOB
MICHELE LAROQUE
Illustration Robert WAGT
Un film écrit et réalisé par
FLORENCE QUENTIN
GARANCE CLAVEL
ISABELLE CANDELIER
ALESSANDRA MARTINES
YVAN LE BOLLOC'H
SAMUEL LABARTHE
SERGE HAZANAVICIUS
Avec la participation de
STEPHANE AUDRAN
et JULIEN GUIOMAR
Conseiller Technique PASCAL GENNESSEAUX
Image BRUNO DE KEYZER
Montage ANNE LAFARGE
Direction de la production PHILIPPE DESMOULINS et PIERRE D'HOFFELIZE
Produit par PATRICE LEDOUX
Une coproduction GAUMONT - TF1 FILMS PRODUCTION
www.gaumont.fr

 ABOVE left › Chipie, Agency: Anapurna (Fr) right › NOEL 03, PartDieu Agency: EURO RSCG ENSEMBLE (Fr) BELOW › JAMBES, Virginie (Fr)

soldes

Axa assurancy, Agency: Dreamteam (Fr)

DOMINIQUE

DONOIS FRANCE

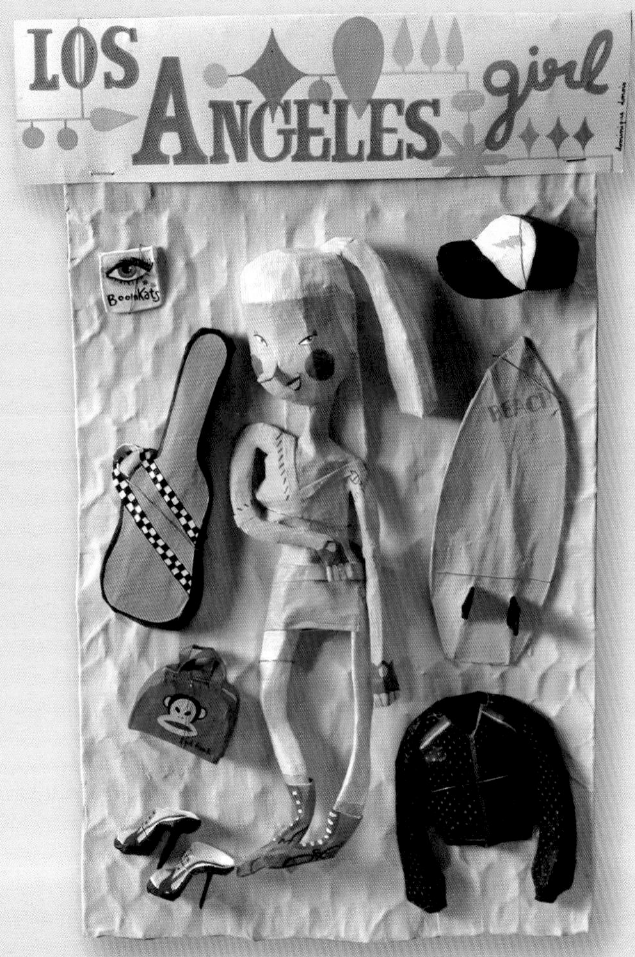

World's Girls, Le Bon Marché, Paris

Anvers girl

TOKYO girl

NEW YORK girl

LONDON girl

THIS PAGE › the "Sappeur", Fashion shop "Destination" New York OPPOSITE › elegant woman, Fashion shop "Destination" New York

ÉLÉGANTE
et accessoires
Paris
Paris
St. Moritz
ROMA
GRAN HOTE
NEW YORK
Paris

the summer outfit, the autumn suit, the winter suit, Fashion shop "Destination" New York

Tokyo Girl, fashion shop "Central Block" Paris

Mao's Soldier, personal work

 Parisian girl, fashion shop "Central Block" Paris

Culotte et Doudou, personal work

Aperitif" scene, Workshop fashion fair NY

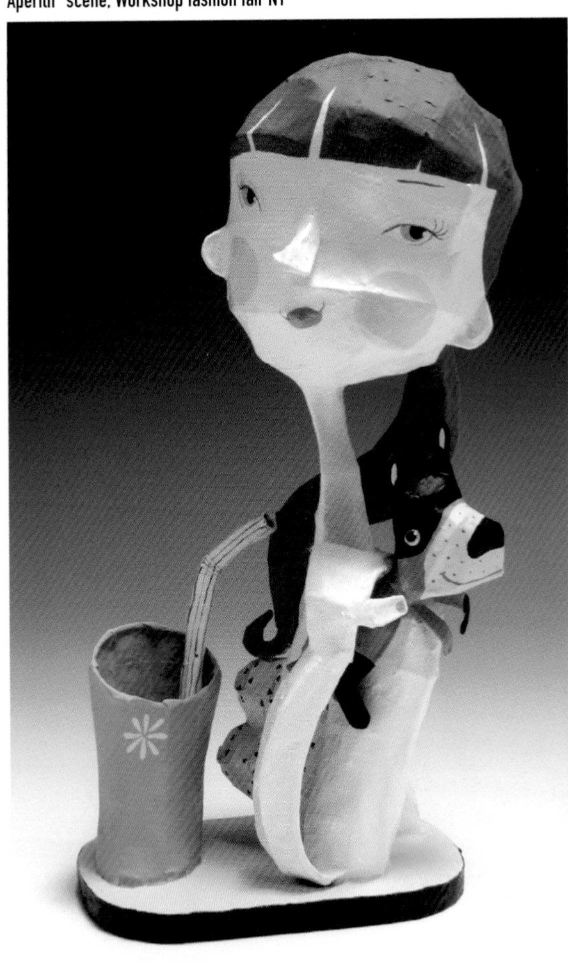

the umbrella, Fashion shop "Destination" New York

UK

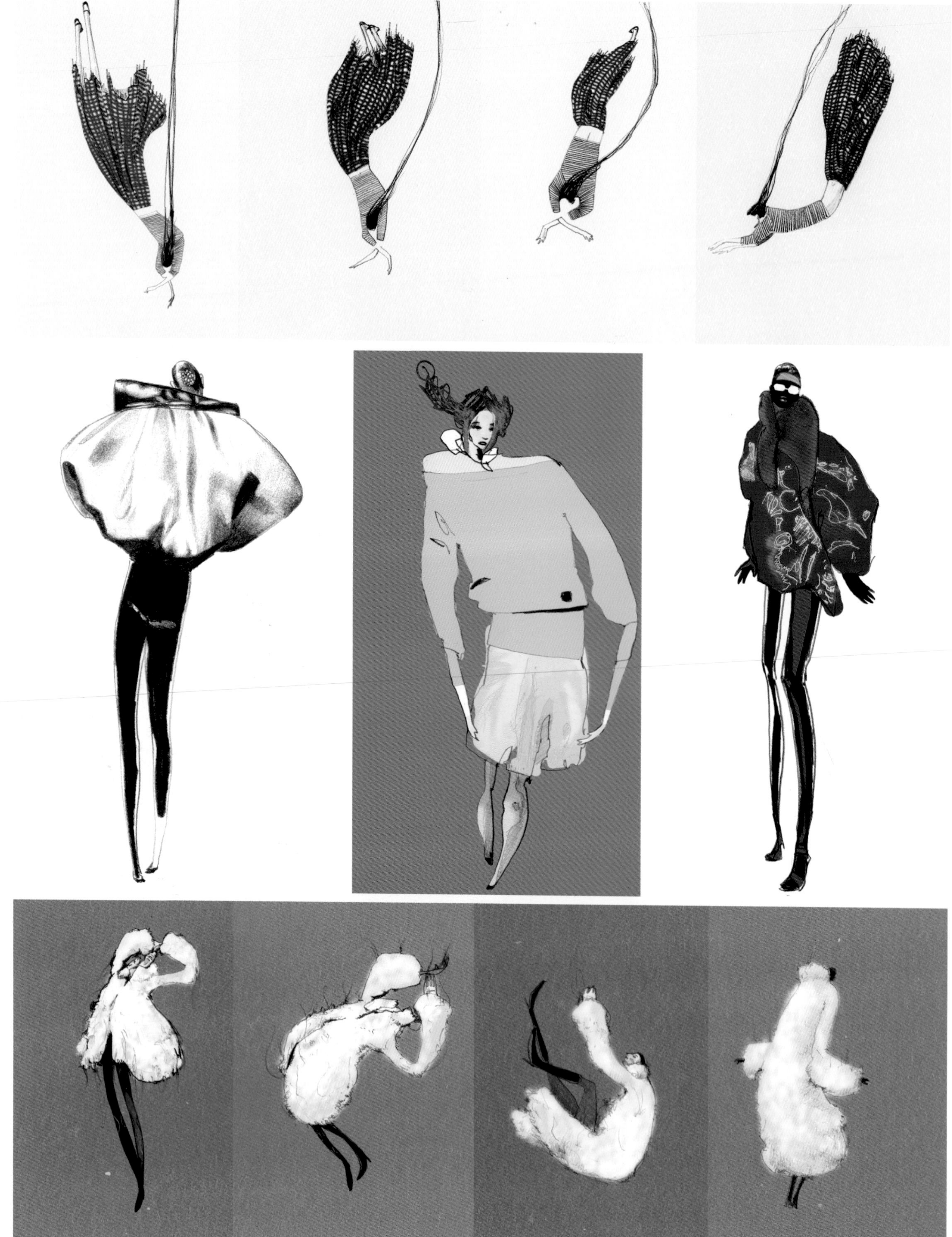

THIS PAGE › Lemon Sorbet, personal work

OPPOSITE
ABOVE › Junya Watanabe – 'Falling for', flash animation, Hintmag.com
MIDDLE LEFT › Viktor & Rolf, personal work
MIDDLE › Viktor & Rolf, personal work
MIDDLE RIGHT › Christian Dior, personal work
BELOW › Alexander Mc Queen – 'Falling for', flash animation, Hintmag.com

'Falling for', flash animation, Hintmag.com – 1. Viktor & Rolf 2. Rochas 3.+4. Comme de Garçons 5. Rochas 6. Viktor & Rolf 7. Dior Homme 8. Raf Simons

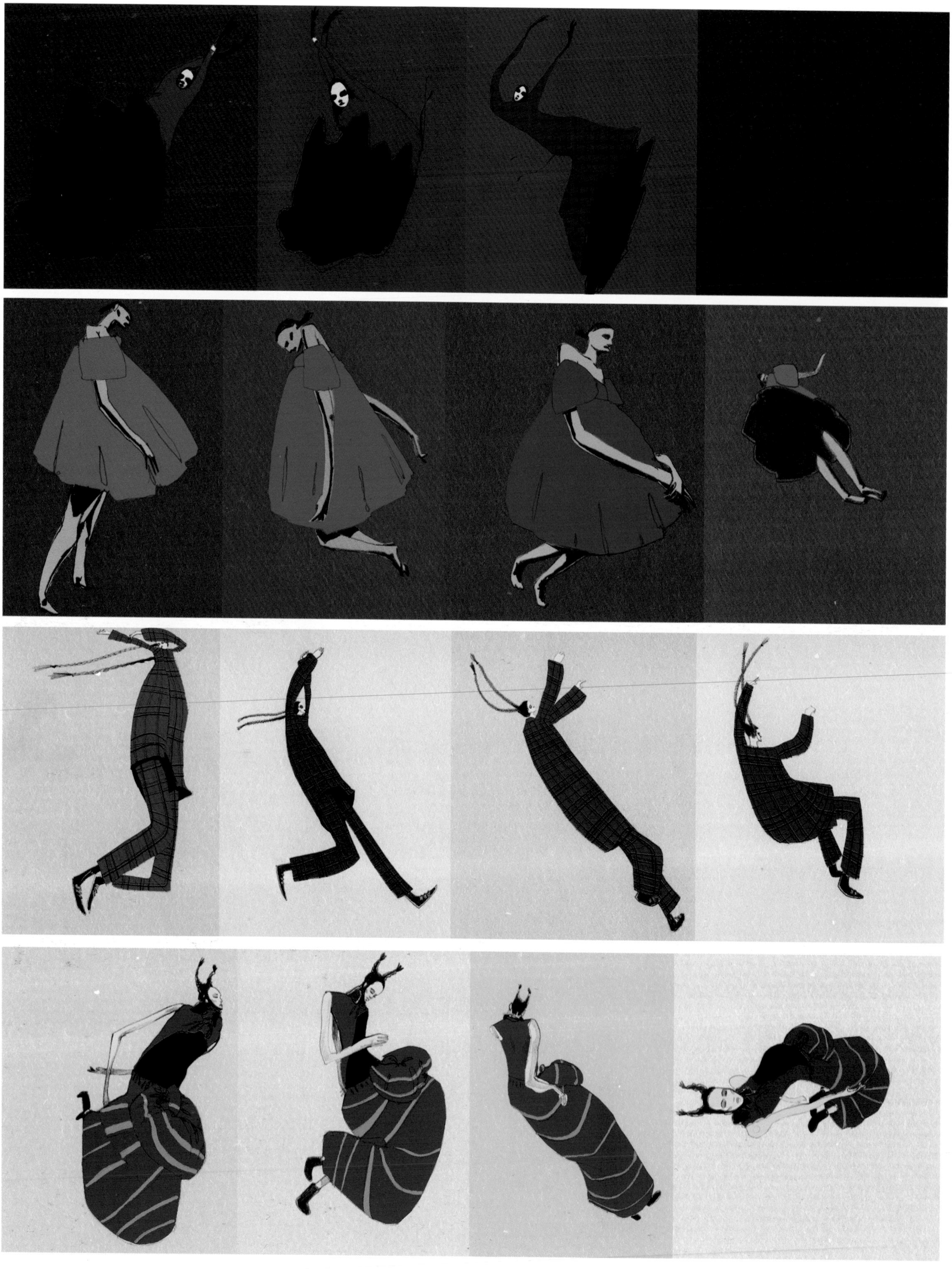

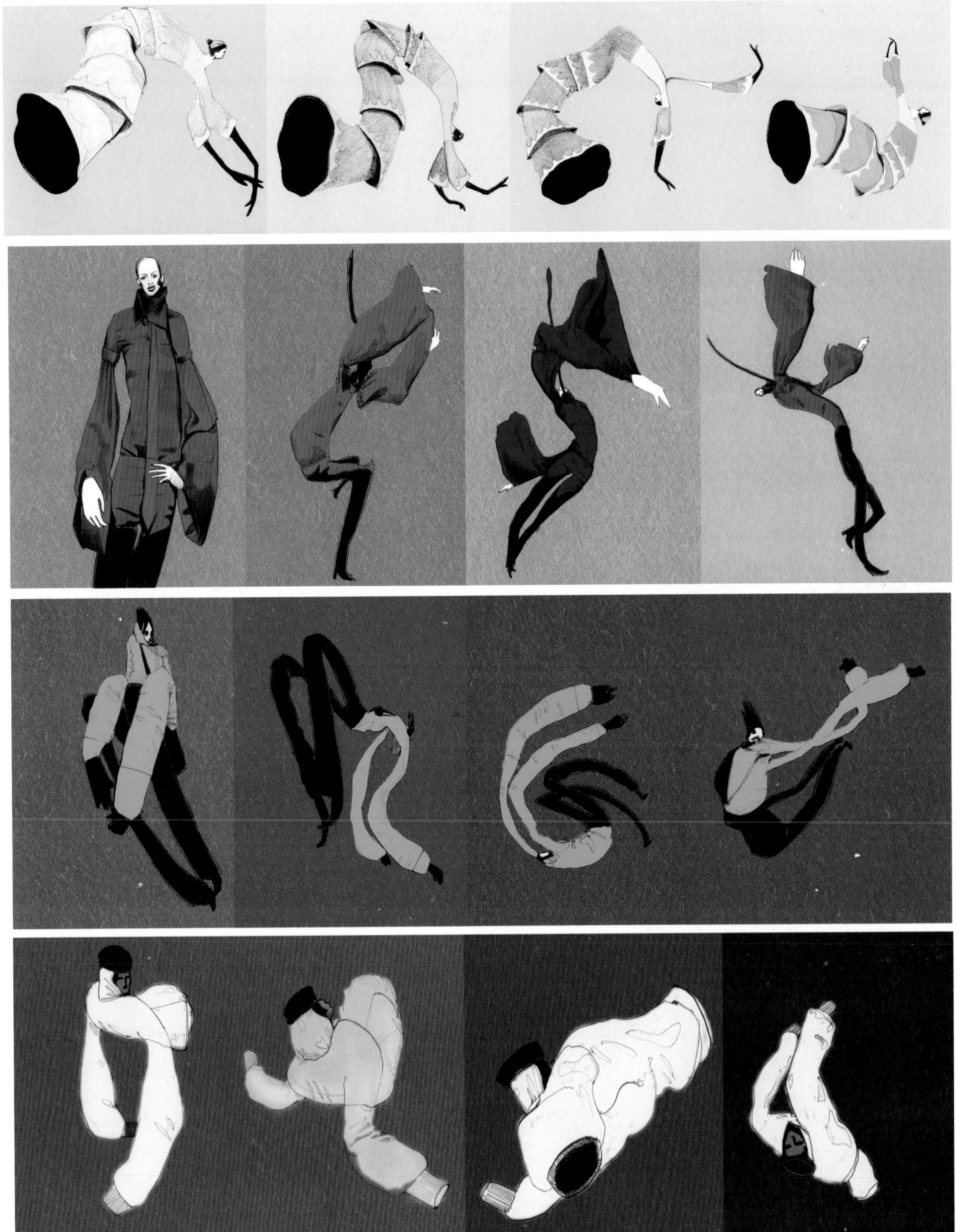

THIS PAGE › image for Hennes, Sweden OPPOSITE › image for The Times

DANIEL EGNEUS

SWEDEN

daniel egneus

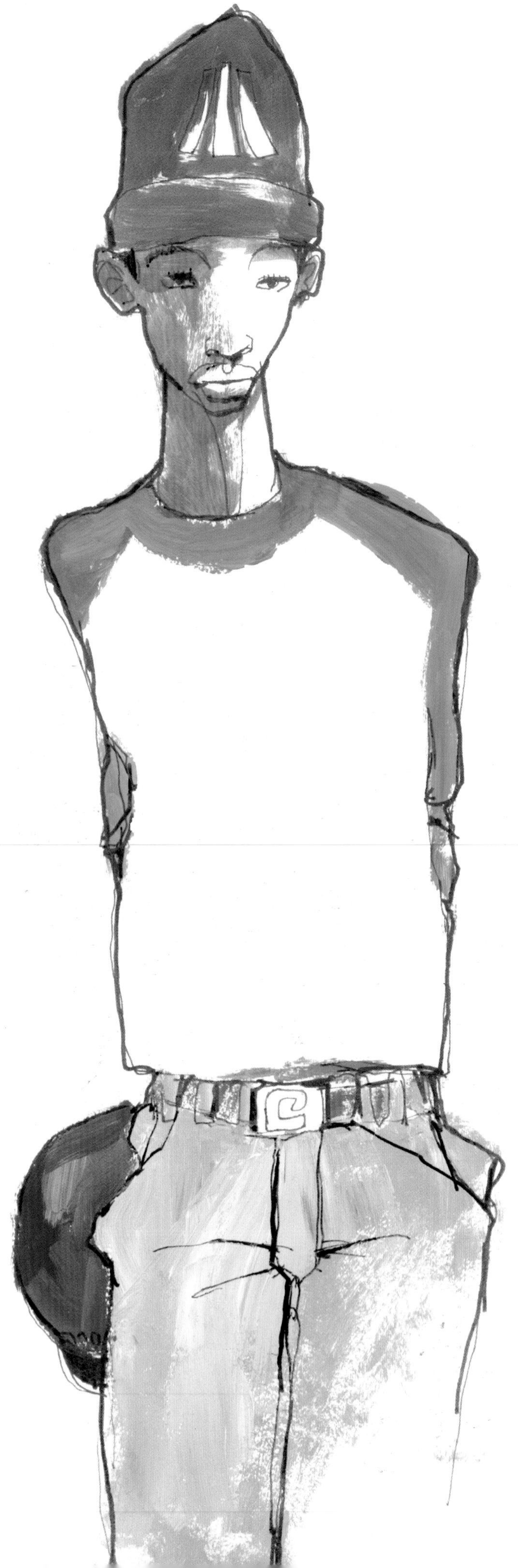

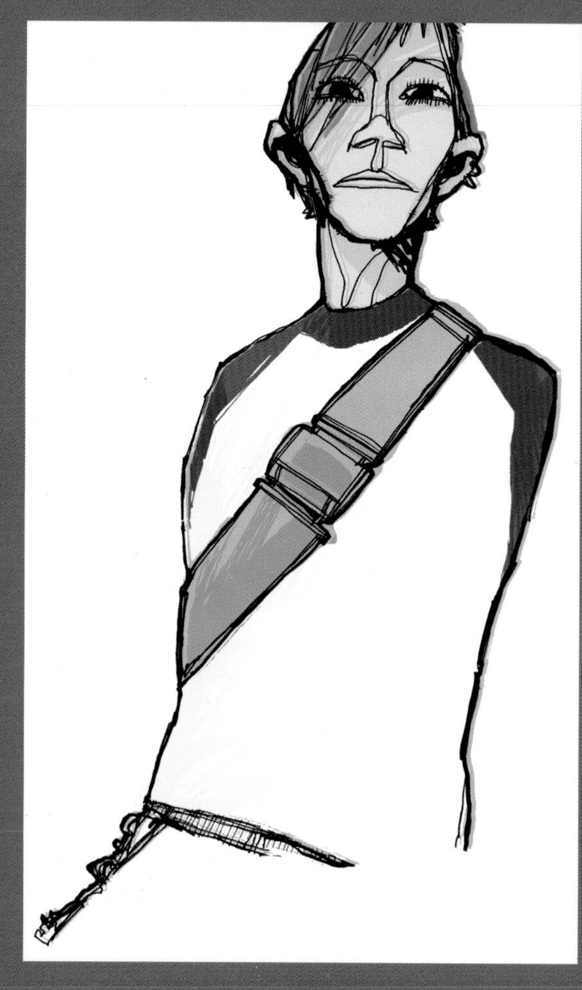

serru
CLES
TRAINS
billets
VIDEO
carhartt®
work in progress - exclusive distributor for europe © 2002 carhartt inc. USA ® carhartt and carhartt logo are registered trademarks of carhartt inc., Dearborn, Mi 48121 U.S.A.

carhartt®

work in progress - exclusive distributor for europe © 2002 carhartt inc. USA ® carhartt and carhartt logo are registered trademarks of carhartt inc., Dearborn, Mi 48121 U.S.A.

carhartt®

work in progress - exclusive distributor for europe © 2002 carhartt inc. USA ® carhartt and carhartt logo are registered trademarks of carhartt inc., Dearborn, Mi 48121 U.S.A.

All the images are made for Carhartt Europe

JONATHAN TRAN UK

the up-rising
maxime vellem
et anteq dignitatis
autroni odio everteretur et in his
splendorem et post
OURS
cum huius periculi propulsatione
sole comfort

 ABOVE left › collapsingstar, peronal work right › imode – Media and Marketing Magazine BELOW › enjoy, peronal work

armsfolded, personal work

SMOOTH CREAMED SMIRNOFF
A COMPLEX FLAVOURED VODKA

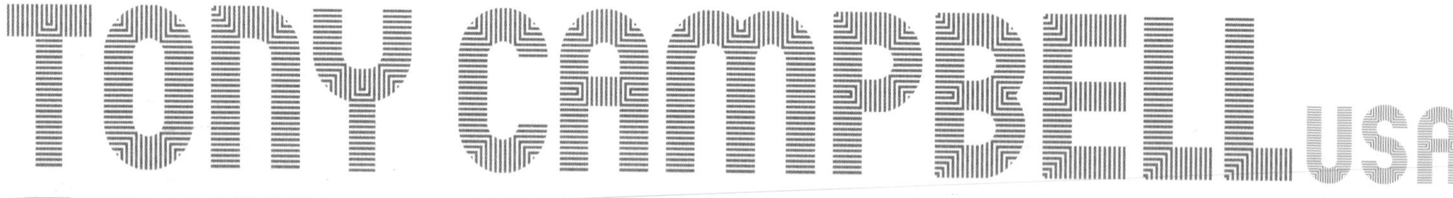
TONY CAMPBELL USA

HOT FIERY BLOODY SMIRNOFF
A COMPLEX FLAVOURED VODKA

PUMA®
Limited Edition
SO DON'T WEAR THEM OUT.
PUMA

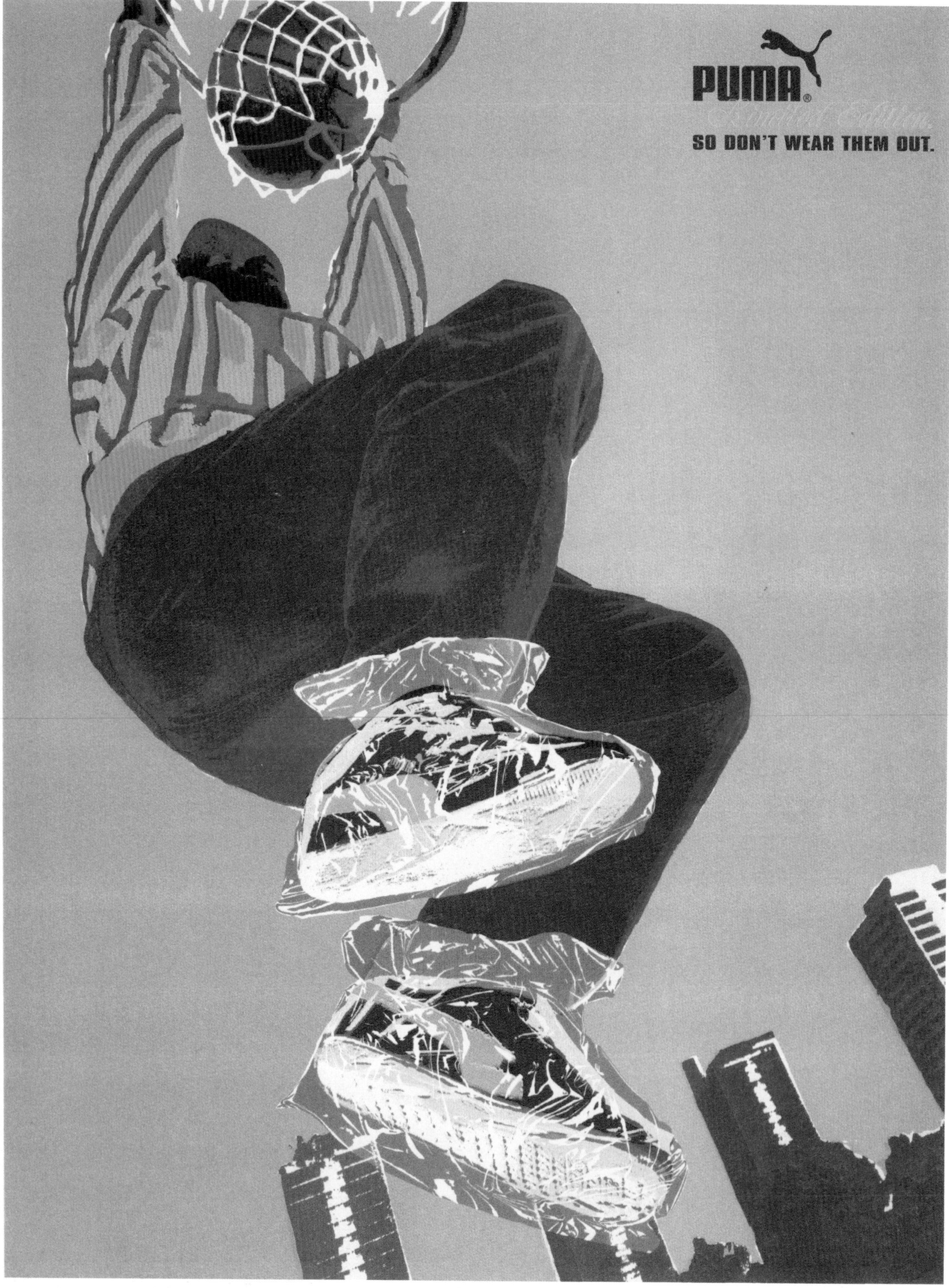
PUMA®
Limited Edition.
SO DON'T WEAR THEM OUT.

PUMA®
Limited Edition.
SO DON'T WEAR THEM OUT.

POLAND

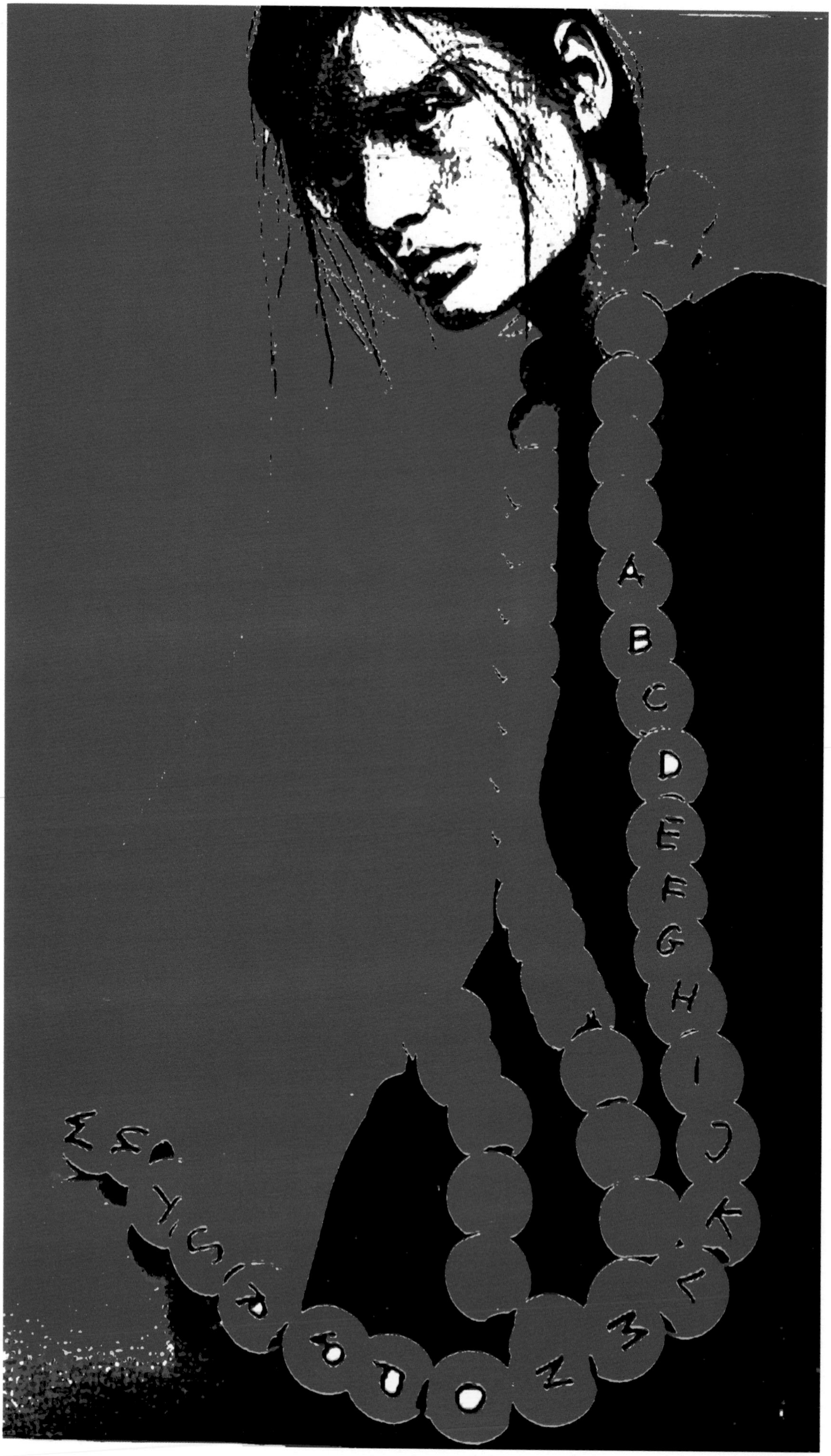

J & M DAVIDSON

AUTUM / WINNTER 2003-04

aga baranska

THIS PAGE › left: Clhoe, trendzine right above: Ida, personal work right below: June, london exhibition OPPOSITE › Kaxia, J&M Davidson

J & M DAVIDSON
GALLERY

THIS PAGE › flower girls, fictive characters OPPOSITE › splash, OUI magazine (bride dress & fashion)

THIS PAGE › above: vœux 2004, personal work below Barbara (left) & Sheryl (right): characters of a serie called "beautiful people" OPPOSITE › lady, character of a serie called "beautiful people"

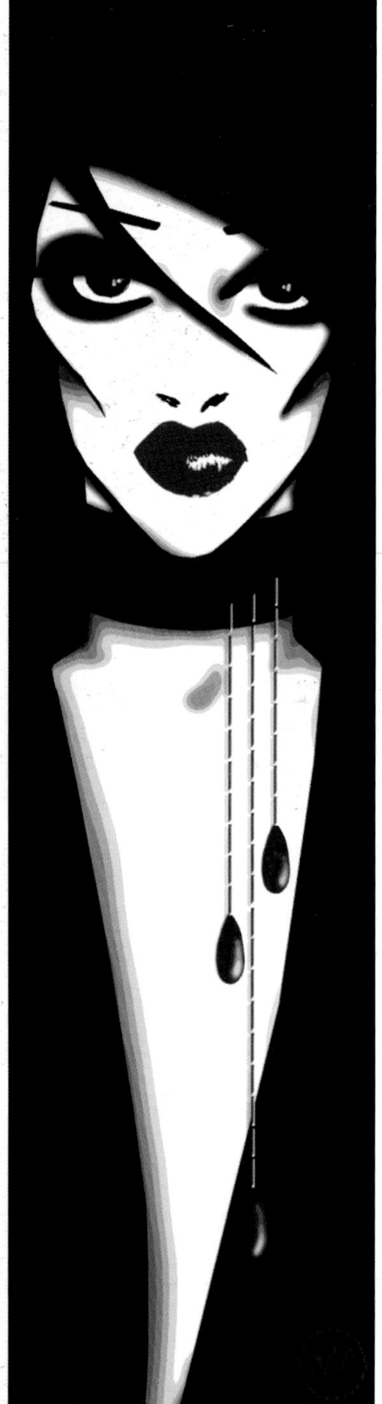

THIS PAGE › above: Scenes d'interieur 1 & 2, poster for a design & decoration exhibition below: Bob 6 man in Red: characters, personal works OPPOSITE › – Red forest, OUI magazine (bride dress & fashion)

 THIS PAGE › left: Bound, accessorizes-catalog right: Legging, accessorizes-catalog OPPOSITE › Mani, character of a serie called "beautiful people"

JACQUI PAULL UK

The Lounge, Personal Work

ABOVE › We are - Personal Work BELOW › cool - Personal Work

 ABOVE > left: Richard Long, Personal Work ABOVE > right: The Eat, Personal Work BELOW > BillBoard, Personal Work OPPOSITE > the Bar, Personal Work

hooker.

THIS PAGE ABOVE › How To Meet Someone, Guardian Weekend Magazine MIDDLE › Excess In The City, Timeout London BELOW › Big Brother 3, And The Winner Is... Channel 4, Guardian Guide
OPPOSITE › Hooker, Sell Yourself EP cover design

CHARLES NICHOLL

THE FRUIT PALACE

THE FRUIT PALACE

CHARLES NICHOLL

THIS PAGE:
ABOVE › Pets, Guardian Weekend Magazine
LEFT › Healthy On The Inside, Guardian Guide
RIGHT › Hunter S.Thomson, Raise Magazine

OPPOSITE:
ABOVE LEFT › Maroc, personal work
ABOVE RIGHT › Dav23, personal work
BELOW: Book front/back cover design for The Fruit Palace, Random House Publishing

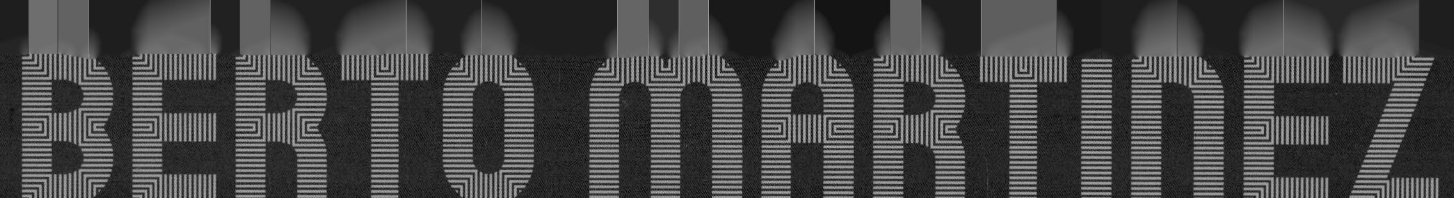

Urban personal work

SPAIN

ABOVE › Warhol, personal work BELOW › Converse, personal work

I ♥ NY

AMERICA

custo®
BARCELONA
Fall/winter 2003-04
Show collection
at the New York fashion week

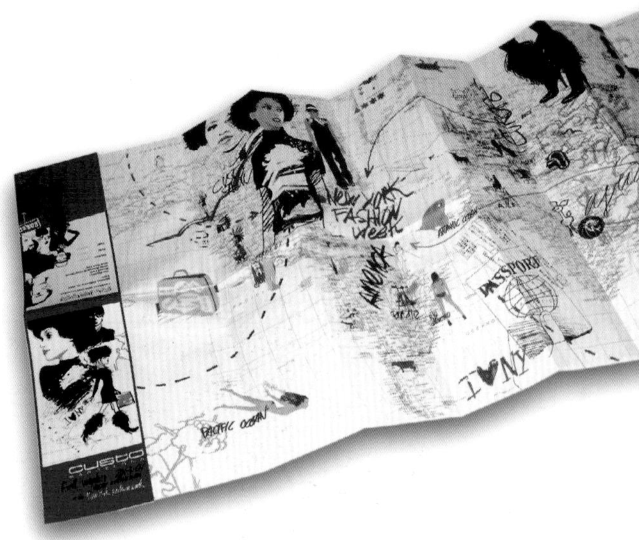

Brochure Custo

CosmoGirl Magazine USA

ABOVE › Various Magazines
BELOW › Optart Dresslab line / Diesel Co.

ABOVE › Casa Brutus Magazine Japan & Woman Magazines
BELOW › Optart Dresslab line / Diesel Co.

ABOVE › Viktor & Rolf personal work BELOW › Dolce & Gabbana personal work

ABOVE › Swingin' London personal work BELOW › Sportmax personal work

VINCENT BAKKUM

FINLAND

ABOVE left › Camille Petit (50x50) right › Cleopatra (50x50) BELOW › Niina smoking (75x50). Agency Lowe et Partners (HKI) OPPOSITE › Red Shoes (60x50). Agency Lowe et Partners (HKI)

 ABOVE › Laura (120x70) BELOW › Niina and Stillife (120x70), Anna magazine

ABOVE left › Niina looking in mirror (70x70) middle › Yello Shoe (50x50) right › Nanouk B. (70x70) BELOW › Niina on the cover of Vogue (70x70)

close
combat

MONTORIOL CASSANDRE

FRANCE

illustration for OFR magazine, france summer 2000

THIS PAGE & OPPOSITE › fashion issue for the website www.d-i-r-t-y.com for DIRTY FASHION photos of Stanislas Wolf

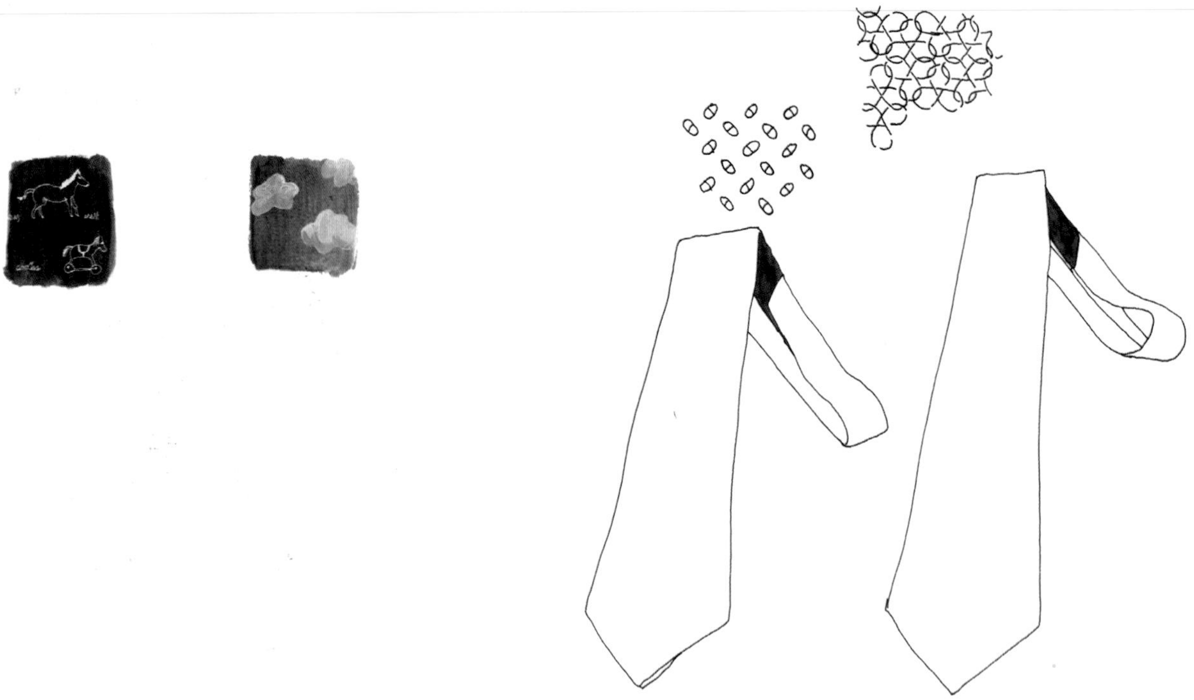

Clamour Silver

cravate en twill de soie imprimé / printed silk twill tie

ABOVE › Common&sense, magazine common&sense, japan 2002 BELOW & OPPOSITE › Hermès, Catalogue Autumn-Winter 2003 bottine-guêtre en box / gaiter-boot in boxcalf

gant en agneau glacé / glove in glazed lambskin

THIS PAGE & OPPOSITE › three of a collection of fashion-based pieces from personal collection

SARAH BEETSON

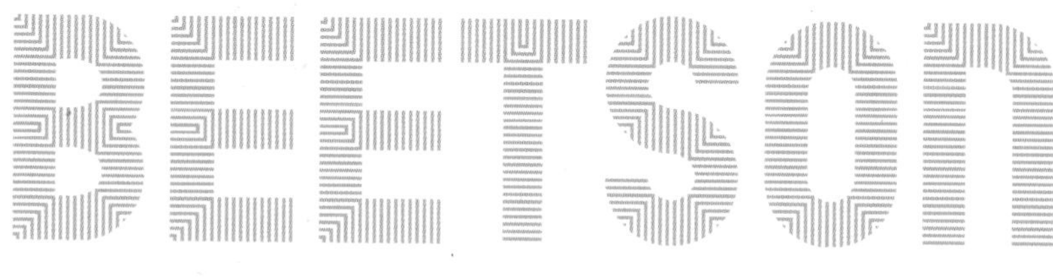

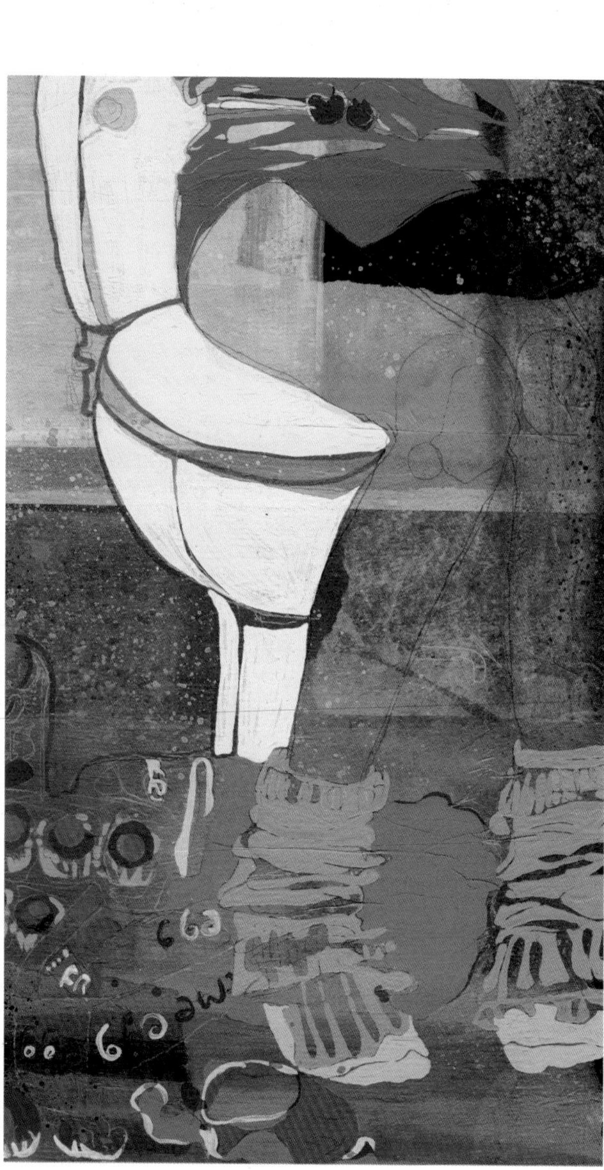

UK

DE SERT BOOT

SOLE CREPE

E
F

DESERT BOOT

03 C0 65 E

PAGES 186-189 › a series of paintings commissioned by clarcks to launch their pure range – shoes made from untreated natural off-white leather

DESERT TREK

1158 66 F

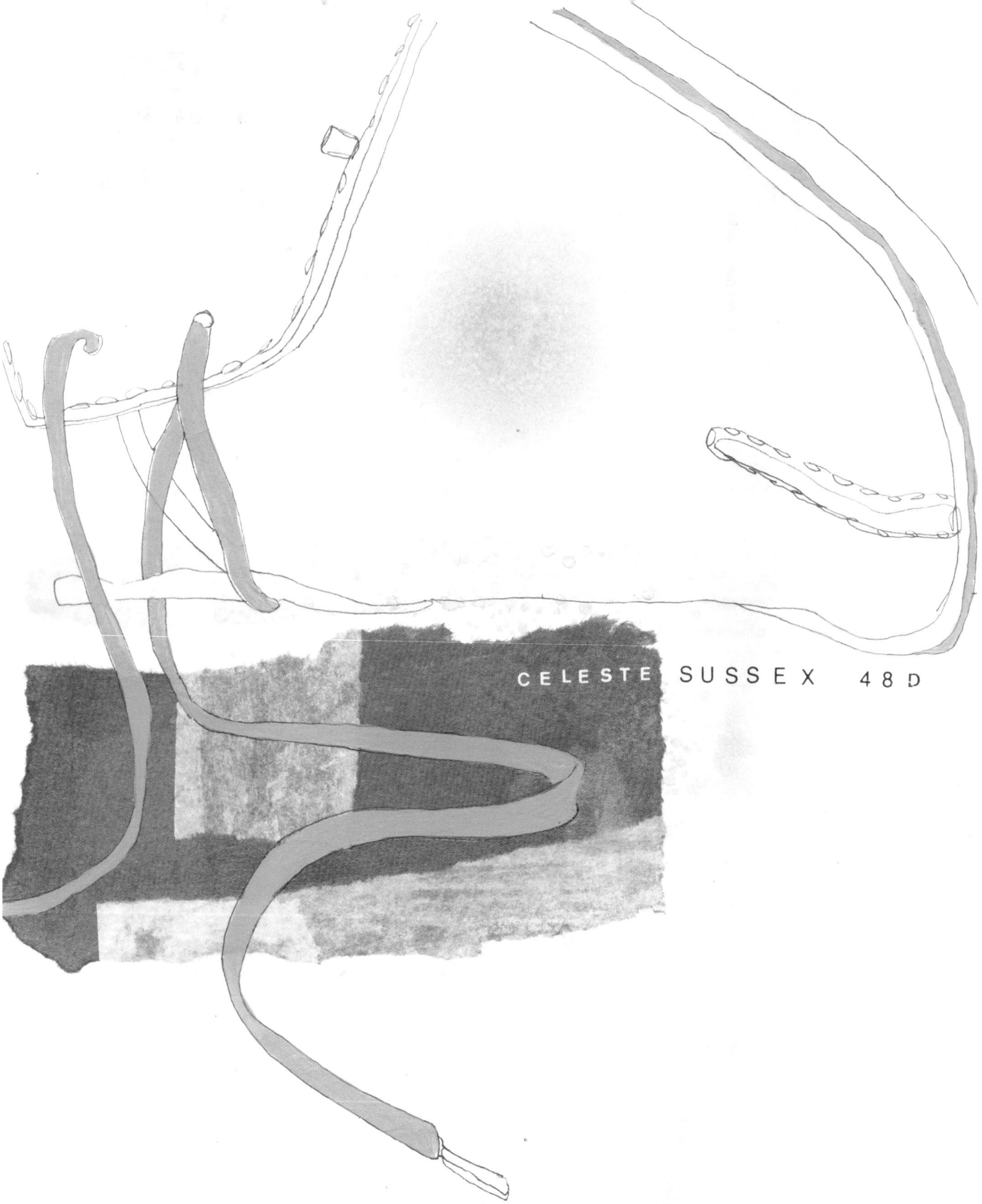

CELESTE SUSSEX 48D

PARTY MONSTER

THIS IS YOUR BRAIN. THIS IS YOUR BRAIN BEING AN ASS.
BY DANIELLE EGAN

"Before I started partying, I was totally black, hated the world," admits Christa*, 19. "Then I met so many cool people, tried ecstasy and I think it saved me from wanting to kill myself on a regular basis."

Sound familiar? Everyone knows there are teens who use drugs and drink, and at least 25 per cent of you "binge"—aren't regular users but go nuts once in a while. Why? Because it makes you feel like you fit in, because for shy people who find it hard to relax, drinking or drugs are time-honoured but not-so-healthy ways to feel more confident. And because, let's be honest, it can be fun. But think it's all giggles and beer goggles? Kinda proud calling friends to say, "Oh my God, I got so loaded last night"? Wrong!

Drinking and doing drugs might seem cool, but if you get loaded, you'll probably come off more like a freak show than a divine diva. Before you take the leap, picture yourself staggering around showing off your underwear, tripping out in a corner and eventually being hoisted into a drunk driver's car. Plus, being bombed can leave you susceptible to the dubious charms of any loser in the room—over half of sexually active teens have unplanned sex while drinking or doing drugs.

"It's unbelievable the things that happen at parties," says Kristina, 18. "A lot of the time, girls try to impress guys, drinking way too much and ending up in emergency." Kristina has even seen messed-up girls having sex with a bunch of boys while the whole thing's being videotaped. "Five minutes later, these guys are making fun of them and looking for their next target," she says.

And if you think a ruined rep is the end of the world, what about the risk of injury, death or feeling like crap for days after? Alannah, 16, used to be a big E and speed popper, but no more. "You're taking a risk every time you do ecstasy," she says, particularly because E can be packed with other stuff like animal tranquilizers or crystal meth. "And the comedown leaves you sketchy and disgusting, such a bitch!" she groans. "The drugs will drag you in and it's hard to get out of it. You should party for the friends and the music, not the drugs."

And sometimes even the initial perceived pluses, like being less wallflowery, wear off. At first, Lisa, 18, used drugs at parties and raves to loosen up and get rolling on the dance floor. "After awhile, I'd get too paranoid and anxious on it and I couldn't dance," she says. "I realized that the total party kids never touched drugs. The best thing is to party straight. When you can't function, you need to think about what you're doing."

Whatever your choices are, make them arriving with all the facts, and always party with a buddy. Knowing what you're taking and having a pact with a close friend that you'll keep an eye on each other goes a long way.

THIS PAGE & OPPOSITE › sketches & illustrations for articles in fashion 18 magazine

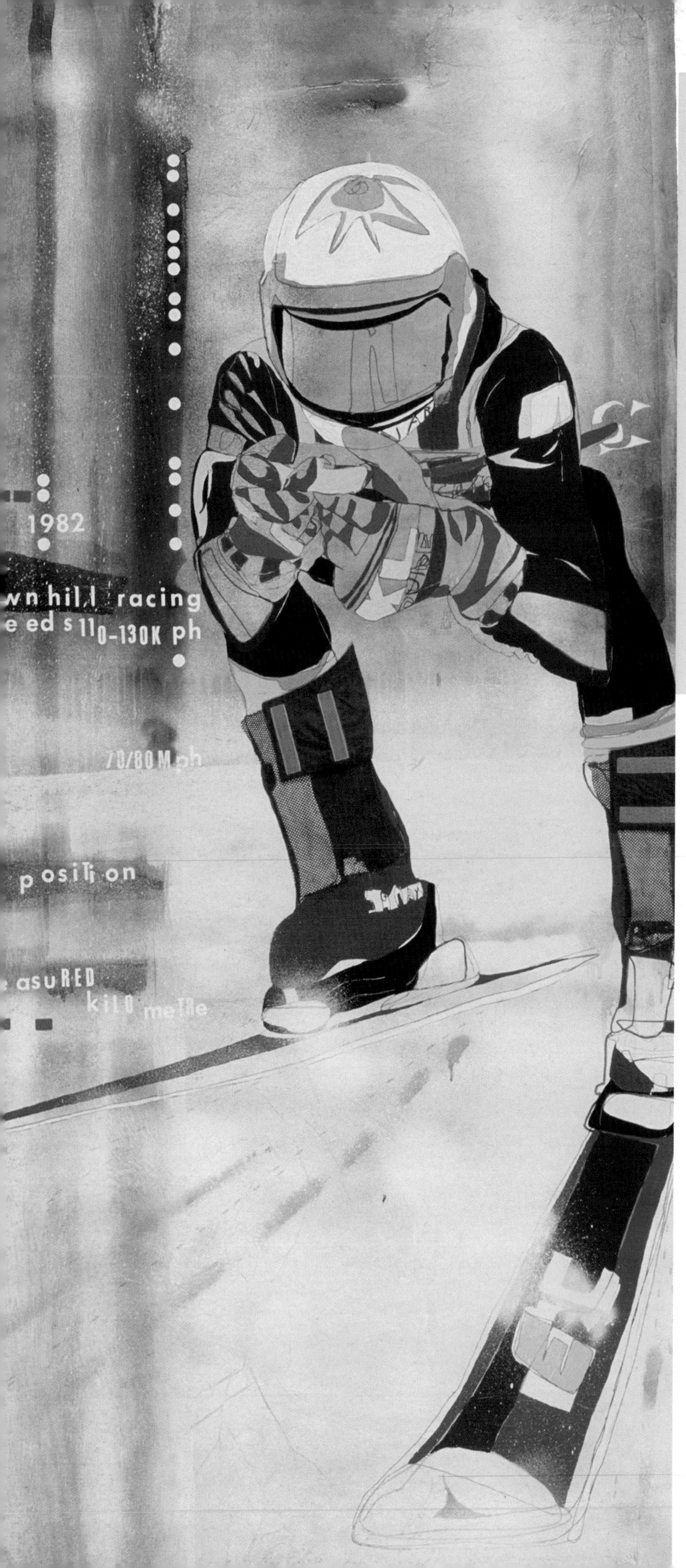

THIS PAGE & OPPOSITE › ellesse pentland awards 2002 1st prize winning Stan Smith piece, followed up with the commission for two life size figures

15 /40
ellesse
PERUGIA · ITALIA

SOPHIE
BOUXOM
FRANCE

THIS PAGE › fashion magazine Gio (italy) OPPOSITE › mes coordonnées, personal work

 ABOVE left › back, personal work right › Japan horoscope gemini, Figaro madame magazine BELOW › Greeting card 2002

ABOVE left › dodo, personal work right › burger queen, personal work BELOW › mademoiselle Chantal, personal work

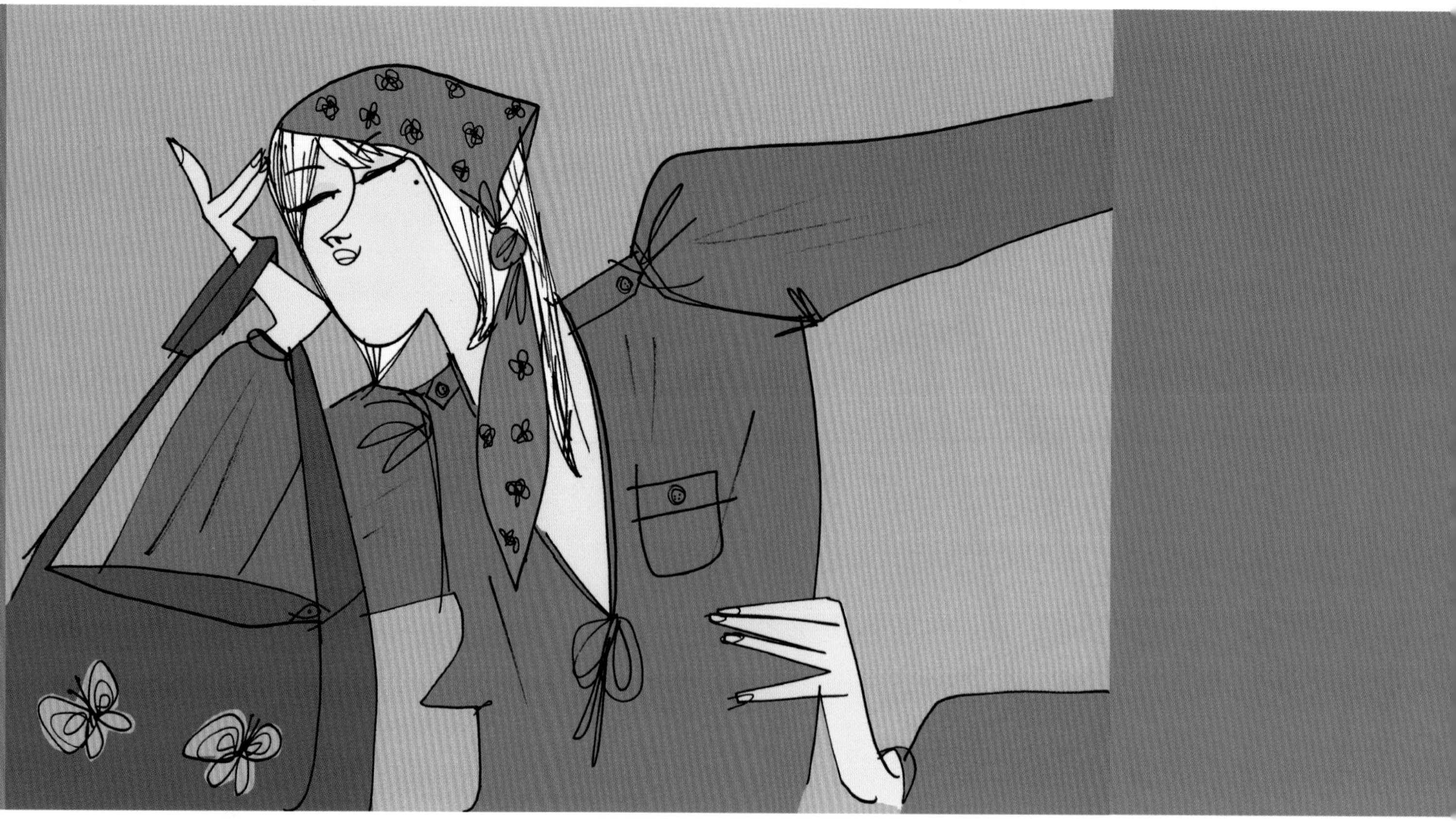

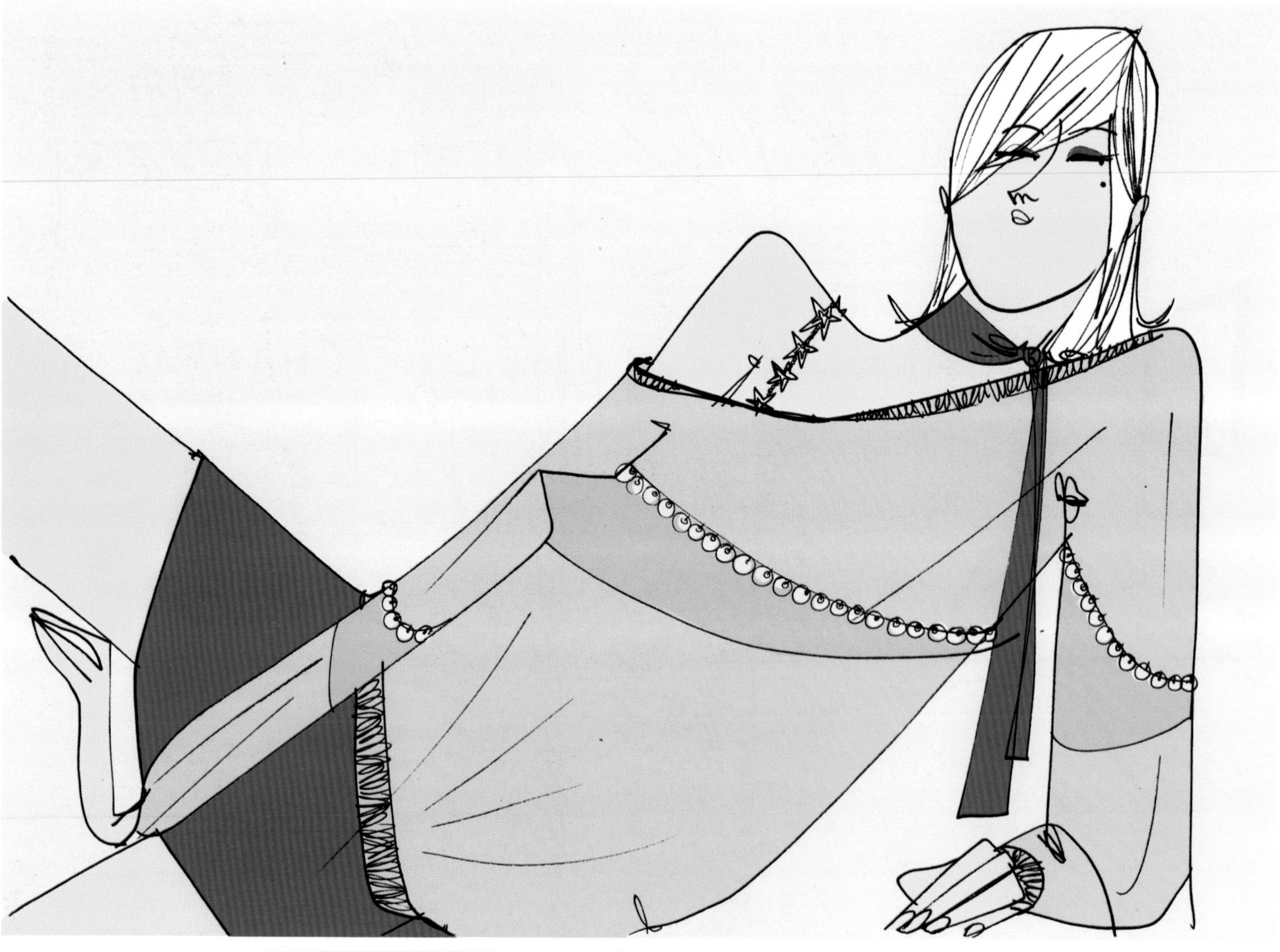

DELICATESSEN

ITALY

THIS PAGE › charme, YOU magazine (uk) OPPOSITE › picnic in autumn, promotional card for kate larkworthy agency

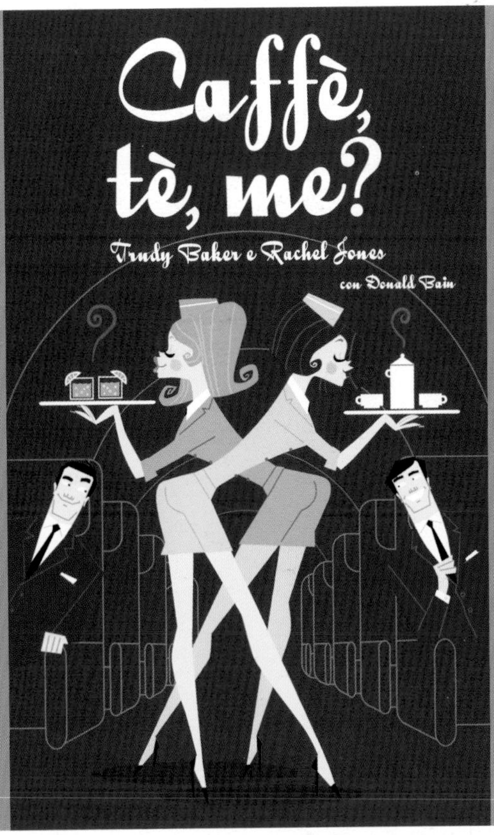

THIS PAGE above left › flora promotional card for kate larkworthy agency right › cover book, sperling & kupfer (italy) below › commitment phobes, YOU magazine (uk) OPPOSITE › blue hotel, personal work

woman trouble, personal work

CONTACTS

TINA BERNING

www.tinaberning.de
tina@tinaberning.de
AGENT:
CWC International, Inc. U.S.A.
296 Elizabeth St. #1F, New York
PH: +(1) 646-486-6586
email: agent@cwc-i.com
web: www.cwc-i.com/
FOR ASIA
Cross World Connections, Ltd. JAPAN
PH: +(81) 3-3496-0745/46
email: agents@cwctokyo.com
web: www.cwctokyo.com
FOR BENELUX: www.artbox.nl

SEB JARNOT

www.sebjarnot.com
contact@sebjarnot.com

AGENT:
Agent 002
70 Rue de la Folie Méricourt
75100 Paris, France
PH: 33 -(0)1 40210348
FAX: 33 -(0)1 40210349
www.agent002.com
valerie@agent002.com

UNIT C.M.A (NY & Amsterdam)
www.unit.nl

TOBIE GIDDIO

www.tobiegiddio.com
tobie@tobiegiddio.com

AGENT:
CWC International, Inc. U.S.A.
296 Elizabeth St. #1F, New York
PH: +(1) 646-486-6586
email: agent@cwc-i.com
web: www.cwc-i.com/
FOR ASIA
Cross World Connections, Ltd. JAPAN
PH: +(81) 3-3496-0745/46
email: agents@cwctokyo.com
web: www.cwctokyo.com

KENZO MINAMI

kenzo@panoptic.org

AGENT:
CWC International, Inc. U.S.A.
296 Elizabeth St. #1F, New York
PH: +(1) 646-486-6586
email: agent@cwc-i.com
web: http://www.cwc-i.com/
FOR ASIA
Cross World Connections, Ltd. JAPAN
PH: +(81) 3-3496-0745/46
email: agents@cwctokyo.com
web: www.cwctokyo.com

KUSTAA SAKSI

www.kustaasaksi.com
kustaa@kustaasaksi.com

AGENT EUROPE:
UNIT
PH: +31 20 530 6000
www.unit.nl

AGENT USA:
UNIT
PH: +1 212 529 0400
www.unit-nyc.com

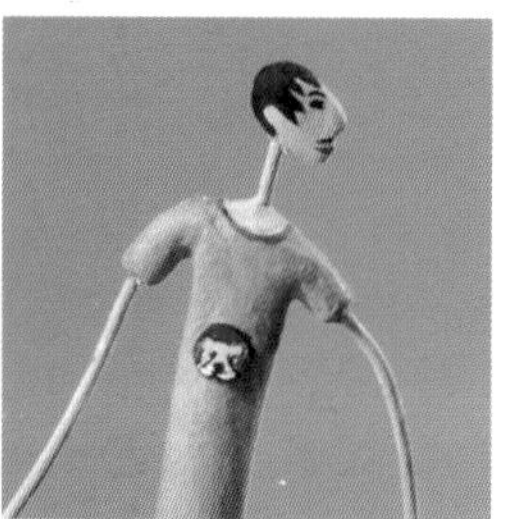

JEAN-MARIE ANGLES

www.adn23.biz/jmangles
j-m.angles@wanadoo.fr

AGENT:
Illustrissimo
33, rue du Faubourg du Temple
75010 Paris France
PH: 01 42 02 50 85
FAX 01 42 02 50 8

www.illustrissimo.com
michel@illustrissimo.com

PIERRE-LOUIS MASCIA

pierre.louis@online.fr

AGENT EUROPE:
UNIT
PH: +31 20 530 6000
www.unit.nl
AGENT USA:
UNIT
PH: +1 212 529 0400
www.unit-nyc.com
AGENT JAPAN:
Jeux de Paume
PH: +81 3 34 86 0532
www.paumes.com

TSUYOSHI HIRANO

AGENT:
chezantoine - Creative management
Antoine Rayssac
5, rue Volta 75003 Paris, France
PH: 33 1 42 78 07 72
www.chezantoine.com
info@chezantoine.com

MARY LYNN BLASUTTA

www.blasutta.com

AGENT FOR FRANCE ONLY
Virginie Challamel
PH: 01 56 98 07 08
FAX 01 56 98 07 17
www.virginie.fr
virginie@virginie.fr

PIET PARIS

pietparis@xs4all.nl

AGENT EUROPE:
UNIT
PH: +31 20 530 6000
www.unit.nl

AGENT USA:
UNIT
PH: +1 212 529 0400
www.unit-nyc.com

DAVID BRAY

David.Bray@pvuk.com

AGENT:
PVUK
8 North Hermitage Belle Vue
Shrewsbury, Shropshire
SY3 7JW U.K.
PH: +44 (0) 1743 350 355
Fax: +44 (0) 1743 289 384

www.pvuk.com
create@pvuk.com

STINA PERSSON

www.tobiegiddio.com
tobie@tobiegiddio.com

AGENT:
CWC International, Inc. U.S.A.
296 Elizabeth St. #1F, New York
PH: +(1) 646-486-6586
email: agent@cwc-i.com
web: http://www.cwc-i.com/
FOR ASIA
Cross World Connections, Ltd. JAPAN
PH: +(81) 3-3496-0745/46
email: agents@cwctokyo.com
web: http://www.cwctokyo.com

MAXIME TOURATIER

AGENT:
chezantoine - Creative management
Antoine Rayssac
5, rue Volta 75003 Paris, France
PH : 33 1 42 78 07 72
www.chezantoine.com
info@chezantoine.com

JACQUELINE WHITE

missjacquelinewhite@hotmail.com

AGENT:
CHIA LIMITED
85 Barlby Road, London, W10 6BN,
England
PH: ++44208 962 1801

www.chiastudio.com
agency@chiastudio.com

ROBERT WAGT

AGENT USA :
LINDGREN& SMITH
630, Ninth Avenue (suite 801)
New York,NY 10036
PH: 212 397 7330
www.lindgrensmith.com

AGENT EUROPE:
VIRGINIE
5, rue de Charonne
75011 Paris
PH: 01 56 98 07 08
www.virginie.fr

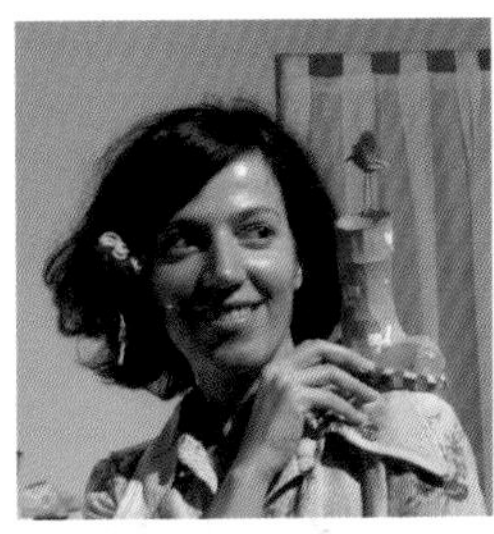

DOMINIQUE DONOIS

dominiquedonois@yahoo.fr

AGENT:
TIPHANIE
110 rue des Grand champs
75020 Paris, France
PH+FAX: 33 (01) 43725091

www.tiphaine-illustration.com
tiphaine@tiphaine-illustration.com

CHRIS GAMBRELL

gambrellchris@aol.com

AGENT:
Agent 002
70 Rue de la Folie, Méricourt
75100 Paris, France
PH: 33 -(0)1 40210348
FAX: 33 -(0)1 40210349

www.agent002.com
valerie@agent002.com

DANIEL EGNEUS

www.danielegneus.com
daniel@danielegneus.com

AGENT:
Thorogood illustration
5 dryden street, covent garden
london wc2e 9nw, united kingdom
PH: +44 (0) 208 859 7507
+44 (0) 208 488 3195
FAX: +44 (0) 208 333 7677

www.thorogood.net
draw@thorogood.net

JONATHAN TRAN

Jonathan.Tran@pvuk.com

AGENT:
PVUK
8 North Hermitage Belle Vue
Shrewsbury, Shropshire
SY3 7JW U.K.
PH: +44 (0) 1743 350 355
Fax: +44 (0) 1743 289 384

www.pvuk.com
create@pvuk.com

ANDY POTTS

AGENT:
Thorogood illustration
5 dryden street, covent garden
london wc2e 9nw
united kingdom
PH: +44 (0) 208 859 7507
+44 (0) 208 488 3195
FAX: +44 (0) 208 333 7677

www.thorogood.net
draw@thorogood.net

TONY CAMPBELL

Tony.Campbell@pvuk.com

AGENT:
PVUK
8 North Hermitage Belle Vue
Shrewsbury, Shropshire
SY3 7JW U.K.
PH: +44 (0) 1743 350 355
Fax: +44 (0) 1743 289 384

www.pvuk.com
create@pvuk.com

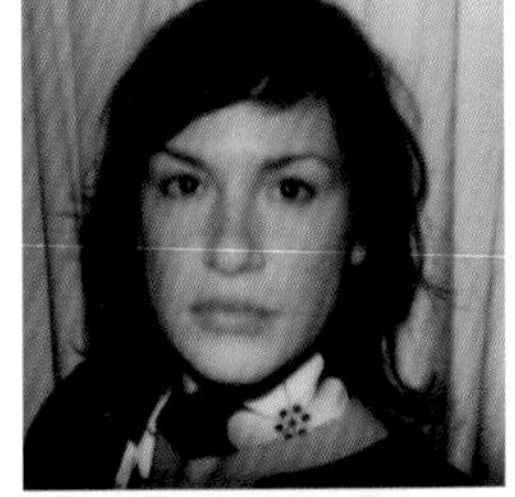

AGA BARANSKA

www.agabaranska.com
agabaranska@yahoo.com

AGENT:
CHIA LIMITED
85 Barlby Road, London, W10 6BN,
England
PH: ++44208 962 1801

www.chiastudio.com
agency@chiastudio.com

MATEO

misyl@noos.fr

AGENT FOR EUROPE:
Agent 002
70 Rue de la Folie Méricourt
75100 Paris, France
PH: 33 -(0)1 40210348
FAX: 33 -(0)1 40210349

www.agent002.com
valerie@agent002.com

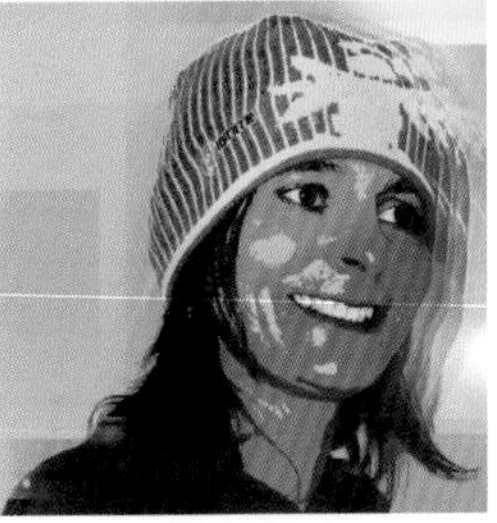

JACQUI PAULL

Jacqui.Paull@pvuk.com

AGENT:
PVUK
8 North Hermitage Belle Vue
Shrewsbury, Shropshire
SY3 7JW U.K.
PH: +44 (0) 1743 350 355
FAX: +44 (0) 1743 289 384

www.pvuk.com
create@pvuk.com

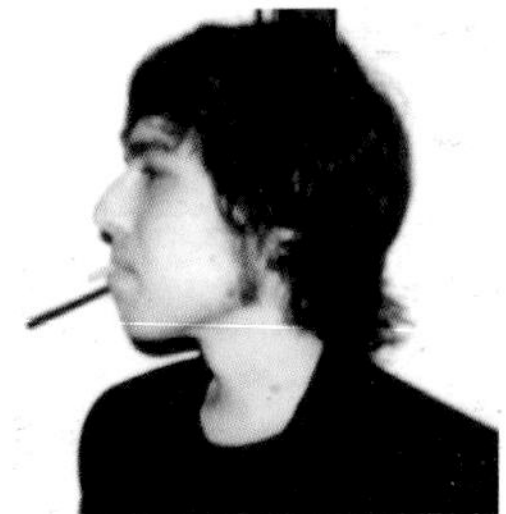

BERTO MARTINEZ

www.bertomartinez.com
joanignasi@bertomartinez.com

AGENT FOR EUROPE:
Agent 002
70 Rue de la Folie Méricourt
75100 Paris, France
PH: 33 -(0)1 40210348
FAX: 33 -(0)1 40210349
www.agent002.com
valerie@agent002.com

AGENT FOR JAPAN
Kasumi Ozeki, Taiko & Associates,
www.ua-net.com

VINCENT BAKKUM

vincent.b@kolumbus.fi

AGENT:
Agent 002
70 Rue de la Folie, Méricourt
75100 Paris, France
PH: 33 -(0)1 40210348
FAX: 33 -(0)1 40210349

www.agent002.com
valerie@agent002.com

MONTORIOL CASSANDRE

www.cassandrem.com
cassandre.m@noos.fr

AGENT:
Agent 002
70 Rue de la Folie, Méricourt
75100 Paris, France
PH: 33 -(0)1 40210348
FAX: 33 -(0)1 40210349

www.agent002.com
valerie@agent002.com

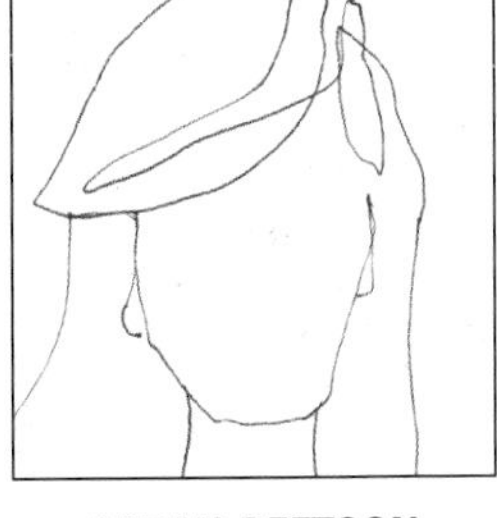

SARAH BEETSON

sarahbeets@hotmail.com

AGENT:
Illustration
United Kingdom
2 Brooks Court,
Cringle Street, London. SW8 5BX

PH: +44 (0)20 7720 5202
FAX: +44 (0)20 7720 5920

www.illustrationweb.com
team@illustrationweb.com

SOPHIE BOUXOM

sophie@hartlandvilla.com

AGENT:
Agent 002
70 Rue de la Folie, Méricourt
75100 Paris, France
PH: 33 -(0)1 40210348
FAX: 33 -(0)1 40210349

www.agent002.com
valerie@agent002.com

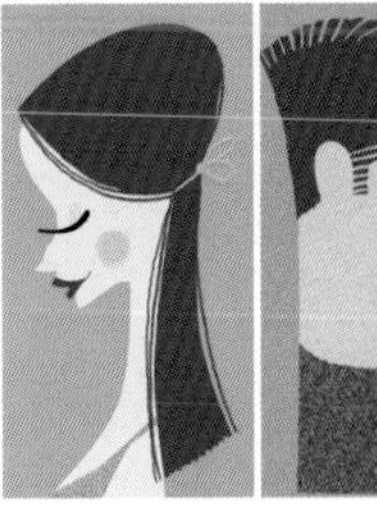

DELICATESSEN

Cristiana Valentini + Gabriele Fantuzzi

www.delicatessen.it
info@delica.it

AGENT EUROPE:
Illustrissimo
PH: 01 42 02 50 85
www.illustrissimo.com
michel@illustrissimo.com

AGENT USA, UK & JAPAN:
KATE LARKWORTHY
ARTIST REPRESENTATION, LTD
182 Norfolk Street #3 New York 10002
www.larkworthy.com
kate@larkworthy.com

MODE 2 courtesy of SLAM JAM Italy www.slamjam.it © Carhartt Europe

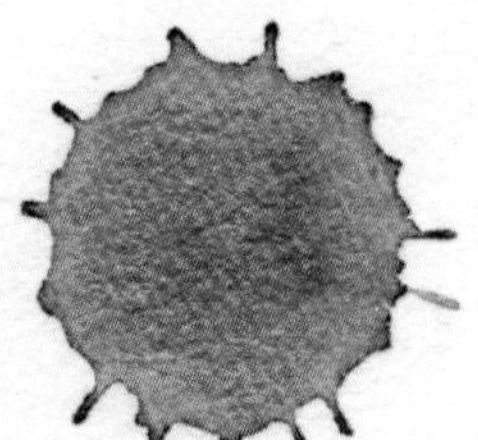

Thanks to all involved in and around FASHIONIZE book, way too many to mention, but you all know who you are...

Tsuyoshi Hirano > Project Japon Ntt/ Docomo. I Mode Kanzai. Osaka

HIRANO.